Cultures at Crossroads

SOUTHEAST ASIAN TEXTILES FROM THE AUSTRALIAN NATIONAL GALLERY

Cultures at Crossroads

SOUTHEAST ASIAN TEXTILES FROM THE AUSTRALIAN NATIONAL GALLERY

18 SEPTEMBER 1992 ~ 17 JANUARY 1993

THE ASIA SOCIETY, NEW YORK

AUSTRALIAN NATIONAL GALLERY, CANBERRA

STUDIES ON ASIAN ART NO. 2

Cover:
(detail) Shouldercloth or man's hipcloth
(salampé; pabasa), cat. 56

Frontispiece:
Ceremonial textile *(tampan)*, cat. 17

Page viii:
(detail) Woman's skirt *(lau pahudu)*, cat. 23

Photograph Credits

Photographs of objects included in the
exhibition were provided by Photographic Services at the
Australian National Gallery.
Supplementary photographs were provided by:
Field Museum of Natural History, Chicago;
Koninklijk Instituut voor de Tropen, Amsterdam;
John Maxwell, Canberra;
Musée de l'Homme, Paris;
Museum of Cultural History, University of California, Los Angeles;
National Museum, Phnom Penh.

Cataloguing-in-publication data

Australian National Gallery.
Cultures at crossroads.

Bibliography.
ISBN 0 642 13066 3

1. Australian National Gallery—Exhibitions.
2. Textile crafts—Asia, Southeastern—Exhibitions.
3. Textile crafts—Australian Capital Territory—Canberra—Exhibitions.
I. Title.

746.09590749471

Edited by Graham Grayston
Designed by Georgiana Goodwin
Printed and bound in Mexico by Impresora Donneco International,
a division of R.R. Donnelley & Sons Company.
Australian National Gallery Studies on Asian Art Series editor Michael Brand
© The Australian National Gallery, 1992.

Acknowledgements

Funding for *Cultures at Crossroads* has been made possible by a
grant from the American Friends of the Australian National Gallery (AFANG).
They wish to acknowledge the support of:

MAJOR
FUNDERS

American Argosy Group
Australian Ministry of Foreign Affairs and Trade
L. Gordon Darling AO, CMG
Henry Gillespie
Bernard H. Leser
Merrill Lynch & Co., Inc.
J.P. Morgan & Co, Inc (courtesy of John F. Ruffle)
Victor Smorgon AO
Loti Smorgon AO
Westpac Banking Corporation
and the design contribution of The Condé Nast Publications Inc

ADDITIONAL
FUNDING FROM

Allan Greenway Pty Ltd
Allen, Allen & Hemsley—Australian Lawyers (Sydney/New York)
ANZ Bank
Everett F. Horgan
Mr and Mrs Herman Iskandar
L. William Lane Jr
Edward Merrin
John E. Merow
Mrs Kartini Muljadi
Ralph E. Ogden Foundation, Inc
Cynthia Hazen Polsky
David Salman
Sapura Holdings
Mr and Mrs Geo. T. Scharffenberger
Mrs Soedarpo Sastrosatomo
Benno C. Schmidt AO
Sime Darby Berhad
Ezekiel Solomon
Tanjong P L C
James H. W. Thompson Foundation
Tilleke & Gibbins—Advocates & Solicitors
Anthony J. Walton
Donald Zilkha

ACKNOWLEDGEMENTS
SHOULD ALSO BE MADE
FOR THE VERY GREAT
HELP GIVEN BY
MEMBERS OF THE
AFANG INTERNATIONAL
COMMITTEE FOR THE
EXHIBITION INCLUDING

Ruth N. Barratt
Barbara Evans Butler
Jill Ker Conway
Chantal Curtis
L. Gordon Darling
Helen Ibbitson Jessup
Hon Jack W. Lydman
Hon Edward E. Masters
Hugh M. Morgan
Cynthia Hazen Polsky
Jane Purnananada
Lady Primrose Potter
Iwan Tirta
Raja Fuziah bte Raja Tun Uda
Pahlavi Shah

Foreword

The Australian National Gallery is the youngest national gallery in the world, having opened its doors to the public in 1982. Although the decision to establish a national gallery was made earlier this century, it was not until the 1950s that Australian material was actively acquired for the national collection. In 1968 the collecting policy was extended to embrace art on a world-wide basis.

In recent years the policies for international collecting have taken increasing account of Pacific and Southeast Asian art. Further, many of our collections now represent specific aspects of the cultural heritage of these regions. The magnificent textiles produced throughout Southeast Asia and the Indian subcontinent, and the fascinating cross-fertilization that has occurred from region to region in the development of motifs and techniques, have been of particular interest. As a result, the Gallery has focused on this area, and we now hold a collection of world importance. The collection was the basis for a major publication and exhibition *Tradition, Trade and Transformation: Textiles of Southeast Asia* organized by Robyn Maxwell at the Gallery in 1990.

To mark the tenth anniversary of the opening of the Australian National Gallery, we are presenting a selection of textiles from our Indian and Southeast Asian collection at the Asia Society Galleries in New York. Although the Gallery has lent many works to exhibitions in the United States over the years, this is the first time a complete exhibition of material from the Gallery has been presented in New York. The exhibition was co-ordinated by a committee headed by Dr Michael Brand, Curator of the Department of Asian Art at the Australian National Gallery, Ms Robyn Maxwell, Associate Curator of Asian Art, and Dr Vishakha N. Desai, Director of the Asia Society Galleries.

Cultures at Crossroads is the initiative of the American Friends of the Australian National Gallery (AFANG), and has been supported by the Council of the Australian National Gallery and the Australian Department of Foreign Affairs and Trade. We would particularly like to acknowledge the active role and unswerving commitment of Mr Bernard Leser, President of AFANG. He has been ably supported by Mr Anthony J. Walton, Vice-President of AFANG, and by Mrs Judith Ogden Bullitt and Mrs Jill Ker Conway, Directors of AFANG. We would also like to thank Mr Richard Woolcott, former Secretary of the Department of Foreign Affairs and Trade, Mr Peter Curtis, Australian Consul-General in New York, and Mrs Curtis, Mr and Mrs L. Gordon Darling, Ms Penny Amburg, Cultural Counsellor, Australian Embassy, Washington, and the many people who assisted this project through AFANG. In particular, we would like to make mention of Ms Marietta Tree, who was involved in the early stages of the project but sadly passed away last year. Marietta Tree was the first president of AFANG and worked tirelessly on our behalf.

In addition, we would like to express our gratitude to those many friends and supporters whose generous donations have played such a vital role in making this exciting project a reality.

Finally, we would like to acknowledge the assistance of the Asia Society in presenting this exhibition, and especially the backing of Mr John Whitehead, Chairman of the Asia Society and the board of trustees. Mr Robert Oxnam, President of the Society, has worked with AFANG since the inception of this project. Without his support and the provision of the Asia Society Galleries this exhibition would not have been held in New York. We would also like to pay tribute to Asia Society Galleries Director Dr Vishakha N. Desai, who served on the curatorial committee for the exhibition and helped with all our arrangements in New York.

BETTY CHURCHER
Director, Australian National Gallery

Preface

In the fall of 1990, we were approached by L. Gordon Darling, a good friend of the Asia Society and the Chairman of the American Friends of the Australian National Gallery (AFANG), to host an exhibition in New York based on the collections of the Australian National Gallery (ANG). The exhibition would celebrate the tenth anniversary of AFANG and highlight the strengths of the ANG's permanent collection. After brief discussions, it was decided to feature the extraordinary Southeast Asian textiles assembled by the ANG in the last decade or so. As one of the finest and most comprehensive collections of its kind in the world, it provides the resources for an unprecedented exhibition of textiles with a strong cultural context.

The exhibition is particularly relevant for 1992. On the occasion of the Columbus Quincentenary, it focuses on the trade connections in the very regions sought by Columbus. Additionally, an exhibition highlighting the international and multicultural framework of a region often regarded by the Western mind as remote and exotic brings fresh perspectives to the understanding of the diverse cultures of Southeast Asia.

From its very inception, *Cultures at Crossroads* has been a collaborative project. The exhibition's curatorial focus on broad cultural interactions between Southeast Asia and the rest of the world as seen in textiles — rather than simply a survey of Southeast Asian textile traditions — was developed jointly by Michael Brand and Robyn Maxwell of the ANG and myself. In this way we have sought to present an exhibition that elevates the purely formal beauty of the textiles to a new level of cultural understanding.

Several other staff members of the ANG — Alan Dodge, Kevin Munn and Alan Froud — have also been indispensable to the success of the exhibition. Without the support of Betty Churcher, Director of the Australian National Gallery, the project could not have become a reality. The staff of the Asia Society Galleries has once again produced miracles under financial constraints: Denise Leidy worked on the installation and the organization of the show; Amy McEwen and Richard Pegg ably handled registrarial details; Becky Mikalson and Merantine Hens-Nolan co-ordinated the publication of the catalogue and exhibition interpretation; Mirza Burgos monitored the logistical and financial details; and Heather Steliga-Chen helped with promotion. Robert Oxnam and Marshall Bouton, our President and Executive Vice President, provided support and thoughtful advice throughout the project. I would also like to thank Rochelle Udell and Kevin Hickey of Condé Nast and Georgiana Goodwin, the designer of the catalogue, for their tireless efforts to produce this lovely volume on time and on budget.

Cultures at Crossroads would not have been possible without the enthusiastic support and commitment of the board members of AFANG. Gordon and Marilyn Darling conceived the project, which was later sustained and nurtured by Bernard Leser and Anthony J. Walton. The persistent determination and hard work of Judith Ogden Bullitt and her international committee ultimately allowed us to move forward with the project.

It is a pleasure to introduce our audience in the United States to the rich and complex world of Southeast Asian textiles with their dazzling colours and intricate patterns. It is our hope that the exhibition will explore the cultural diversity of Southeast Asian societies, and that it will delight the eye and enrich the mind as it encourages all of us to celebrate our own multicultural realities.

VISHAKHA N. DESAI
Director, The Asia Society Galleries

vii

Contents

Cultures at Crossroads:
The Context of a Collection

MICHAEL BRAND

1. Australian Aboriginal painting was the subject of the highly successful *Dreamings* exhibition at the Asia Society Galleries in 1988. See Peter Sutton (ed.), *Dreamings: The Art of Aboriginal Australia* (New York: Asia Society Galleries and George Braziller, 1988).

2. For a full history of this fascinating trade, see C. C. Macknight, *The Voyage to Marege': Makassan Trepangers in Northern Australia* (Melbourne: Melbourne University Press, 1976).

Nandabitta *(1911–1981),*
attributed to Groote Eylandt,
Northern Territory
Makassan prahu *and* trepang curing. *c.1974*
natural pigments on bark
Collection: Australian National Gallery,
Canberra

A modern bark painting by an anonymous Aboriginal artist from northern Australia resonates with the special power of an object imbued with several layers of significance.[1] Few images can better illustrate the full cultural richness of the context in which this exhibition of Southeast Asian and Indian textiles from the Australian National Gallery is set, for this painting preserves a visual memory of trade connections between Aboriginal Australia and Southeast Asia that could predate the European settlement of Australia in 1788 by as much as four centuries. A Makassan *prahu*, a type of sailing vessel that plied the route between Sulawesi (in modern Indonesia) and northern Australia, is shown at the top of the painting above a group of Makassan fishermen boiling, drying and sorting a catch of *trepang* (sea cucumber).[2] That the design of such *prahu* is descended from the Arab *dhow* and that the Makassan fishermen were preparing a delicacy destined mainly for markets in China further highlights the complexity of the international trade that passed through the maritime crossroads of Southeast Asia. The impact of such trade was never purely economic. As will be shown in this exhibition, connections opened up by trade played a vital role in the development of the visual arts throughout Southeast Asia.

Crossroads can be both spatial and temporal. Spatially, a crossroads is the point of intersection between two or more pathways, a point linking different regions and frequently serving as a marketplace for the exchange of goods. However, a crossroads can also be seen in terms of time as the metaphorical point at which a number of options present themselves for any journey into the future. The choice of the word 'crossroads' in the title of this exhibition is particularly apt. On the one hand, the central theme of the exhibition is the interplay between indigenous traditions in the art of Southeast Asia and the external forces that travelled along the historic sea lanes that intersect the region. On the other hand, the Australian National Gallery's decision to form a collection of Southeast Asian textiles, and then to send a selection from it as the Gallery's first exhibition in New York, is a potent symbol of the choices that face Australia itself as it stands at the crossroads of cultural plurality.

The trade routes linking Europe, the Middle East, India, China and Japan that cross Southeast Asia are both long and long-standing. They are not a creation of European exploration but rather one of the prizes of colonial expansion: in fact, it was access to this flourishing Asian trade network that had been the original motivation for Christopher Columbus before he landed in the Americas exactly five hundred years ago. But Southeast Asia — the area now comprising the modern nations of Indonesia, Malaysia, Singapore, Brunei, the Philippines, Vietnam, Cambodia, Laos, Thailand and Burma — was not just a crossroads. As Anthony Reid shows in his essay that follows, this maritime intercourse has served as much to unite the peoples of

Southeast Asia with each other as to open up the region to outside influences. In a similar vein, this exhibition does not seek merely to catalogue the effect of outside influences on Southeast Asian art but also to illustrate the complex cultural interrelationships within the region.

Australia's desire to establish a genuine dialogue with its Southeast Asian neighbours has expressed itself in many forms. Among the most recent projects taking a cultural approach have been the exhibition *Out of Asia*, which investigated the views of ten contemporary Australian artists on Asia and its art;[3] a special issue of the journal *Australian Cultural History* dedicated to Australian perceptions of Asia;[4] a path-breaking conference on the subject of 'Modernism and Postmodernism in Asian Art' recently convened at the Australian National University in Canberra;[5] and, most recently, a new book by Alison Broinowski recording Australian impressions of Asia over the past two centuries.[6] Among long-term projects, however, the formation of a national collection of Southeast Asian textiles at the Australian National Gallery and the establishment of a related research program must rank as one of the most important steps in this process.

Set up by an Act of Parliament only in 1973, and opened in 1982, the Australian National Gallery has had the unique and challenging task of establishing a national collection at the very time that the country's political and economic alliances have been undergoing a revision with profound social and cultural implications. One of its primary goals has been to form a comprehensive and outstanding collection of Australian art, both European and Aboriginal. From the very beginning, however, this mission has been paired with an equally intense search for masterpieces from other parts of the world. This has resulted in a number of areas of excellence in both Western and non-Western art. While the Gallery's holdings of modern American art (especially Jackson Pollock's *Blue poles*, acquired amidst great controversy in 1973[7]) are already well known, one of the goals of this exhibition is to highlight parallel achievements in the field of Asian art.

The collection of Asian art by public institutions in Australia had previously followed the path of European and North American museums, although largely without the assistance of great private benefactors. From the nineteenth century onwards, for example, the Art Gallery of New South Wales in Sydney and the National Gallery of Victoria in Melbourne have built up impressive strengths in Japanese and Chinese art, especially painting and the decorative arts.[8] In contrast, the newly created Australian National Gallery set itself the task of collecting a select group of great Hindu and Buddhist images, primarily in the medium of sculpture. To avoid duplicating the holdings of Asian art in Sydney and Melbourne, it was further decided to place greater emphasis on the art of Southeast Asia and India (and, more recently, the Islamic world). The Gallery's first great successes came under the curatorship of Piriya Krairiksh in the late 1970s, when an important collection of Thai Buddhist sculpture was put together. It was not until 1988, however, that a separate Department of Asian Art was formally established. In 1990 a permanent gallery for the display of an Asian collection now numbering over 1700 items — Nomura Court — was opened.

3. Alison Carroll, *Out of Asia* (Bulleen, Victoria: Heide Park and Art Gallery, 1990).

4. *Australian Cultural History*, no. 9 (1990), edited by David Walker, Julia Horne and Adrian Vickers.

5. The conference organizer, John Clark, is currently compiling a volume of papers delivered at the conference. For a brief report on the conference, see David McNeill, 'Modernism and Postmodernism in Asian Art', *Art Monthly (Australia)*, 40 (May 1991), pp. 13–14.

6. Alison Broinowski, *The Yellow Lady: Australian Impressions of Asia* (Melbourne: Oxford University Press, 1992).

Nomura Court, new permanent home for the Australian National Gallery's Asian collection.

7. For a detailed discussion on the formation of this part of the collection, see Michael Lloyd and Michael Desmond, *The Modern Collection: European and American Paintings and Sculptures 1870–1970 in the Australian National Gallery* (Canberra: Australian National Gallery, forthcoming 1992).

8. Broinowski, *The Yellow Lady*, pp. 165–7.

9. Mattiebelle Gittinger, *Splendid Symbols: Textiles and Tradition in Indonesia* (Washington, DC: Textile Museum, 1979).

10. Although not a member of the committee, Ruth McNicoll (then Curator of Primitive Art — as the position was called at the time — at the Australian National Gallery) played a major supporting role.

11. Robyn Maxwell, *Textiles of Southeast Asia: Tradition, Trade and Transformation* (Melbourne: Oxford University Press, 1990).

An early twentieth-century photograph of a Gaddang woman in central Luzon in the Philippines weaving a long cotton textile on a backstrap tension loom.

Ironically, the decision to embark upon the collection of Indonesian textiles (later expanded to include the rest of Southeast Asia and India) was inspired by an exhibition in the United States. When the Australian National Gallery's founding Director, James Mollison, visited Mattiebelle Gittinger's pioneering exhibition entitled *Splendid Symbols* at the Textile Museum in Washington, DC, in 1979[9] he was struck by the powerful and varied aesthetic of Southeast Asian textiles. Though the first response had been largely aesthetic and intuitive, the Gallery's novel decision to establish an expert committee to oversee the collection process quickly broadened the scope of this unique project. The committee members whom James Mollison brought in from outside the Gallery — the late Anthony Forge (Australian National University), James Fox (Australian National University), John Maxwell (Monash University) and Robyn Maxwell (Monash University, and now Associate Curator of Asian Art at the Gallery)[10] — reflected a broad range of Australian scholarship on Southeast Asia and, even more importantly, an unusually harmonious balance of anthropological and aesthetic concerns.

During the ensuing decade, this advisory committee met frequently to select and, more often, reject items from an ever-increasing flow of textiles. It was disbanded in 1990 after the initial phase of the project had been brought to a magnificent conclusion with Robyn Maxwell's exhibition *Tradition, Trade and Transformation* at the Australian National Gallery and her accompanying book *Textiles of Southeast Asia*.[11] While it is intended to develop the Gallery's Asian collection in a number of new directions over the next decade, Asian textiles will undoubtedly remain an area of special interest both in terms of acquisition and research.

Few other artistic traditions can better challenge some of the inadequacies inherent in the construction of art history in the West. To begin with, Southeast Asian textiles are almost without exception the work of women artists. Fortunately, Asian textiles have not suffered from the implied hierarchy of arts in the West, where sculpture and painting have reigned unchallenged as 'fine arts', while other media such as textiles and ceramics have been classified as 'crafts', an ordering firmly established along lines of both class and gender.[12] It is hoped that *Cultures at Crossroads* will stand as one of the great exhibitions by women artists to be mounted in New York.

For many centuries, textiles have been the primary medium of artistic and cultural communication within Southeast Asia. The same holds true for the sophisticated culture of the coastal cities and for more remote tribal groups. Southeast Asian textiles can be charged with ritual significance in the spheres of both religion and state, and touch on almost every aspect of life and death. They carry meaning through the choice of materials, techniques and designs as well as through individual motifs. The fact that this dominant art form was the prerogative of women artists (regrettably, almost entirely anonymous) is highly significant, for, as Robyn Maxwell notes in her introduction to *Textiles of Southeast Asia*:

Since textile production in Southeast Asia was exclusively the task of women, textiles are able to show history from a different perspective by reflecting a female view of the contact between different cultures and are an alternative to the princely epics of war, succession and dominance. Textiles also remind us that many cultures and traditions existed outside the powerful court centres and kingdoms that dominate most accounts of Southeast Asian history.[13]

Given the widespread currency of textiles as a major art form throughout Southeast Asia, their relevance to the pursuit of art history should be self–evident.

Cultures at Crossroads seeks to explain and illustrate the complex evolution of Southeast Asian textiles. After introductory essays by Anthony Reid and Robyn Maxwell on the overall historical and cultural context of textiles and trade in Southeast Asia, six individual themes will be explored: the continuity of ancient textile traditions; the influence of India on Southeast Asian textiles; Indian textiles for trade; Chinese influences; textiles for the new faiths (Islam and Christianity); and batik, a major technique with many design sources.

In his collection of essays entitled *The Predicament of Culture*, James Clifford included a plea for 'exhibitions that locate themselves in specific multicultured junctures'.[14] Although 'multiculturalism' is most often thought of in Australia with respect to the government policy of incorporating diverse cultural attitudes within the original Anglo–Saxon framework of Australian society, Southeast Asia itself is one of the world's original multicultural melting pots. Many different languages are spoken across this vast region stretching between Australia, India and China by peoples practising everything from localized ancestor worship to the great world religions of Hinduism, Buddhism, Christianity and Islam. Malay, the former *lingua franca* of Southeast Asian trade, includes vocabulary derived from the languages of the Middle East and India as well as from a number of European languages. *Cultures at Crossroads* seeks to explore the textiles of the extraordinary 'multicultured juncture' that is Southeast Asia. It is not a search for authentic relics from a classical moment of a single civilization, but rather the celebration of a cosmopolitan tradition in which ancient materials, techniques, designs and motifs are constantly challenged by the new as part of a continuing interplay between indigenous traditions and external forces.

12. Rozsika Parker, *The Subversive Stitch: Embroidery and the Making of the Feminine* (London: Women's Press, 1984), p. 5. In the past, the Australian National Gallery was also guilty of referring to the Asian collection by the title 'Asian art and textiles', as though the latter were not part of the former.

13. Maxwell, *Textiles of Southeast Asia*, p. 24.

14. James Clifford, *The Predicament of Culture: Twentieth-Century Ethnography, Literature, and Art* (Cambridge, Massachusetts: Harvard University Press, 1988), p. 213.

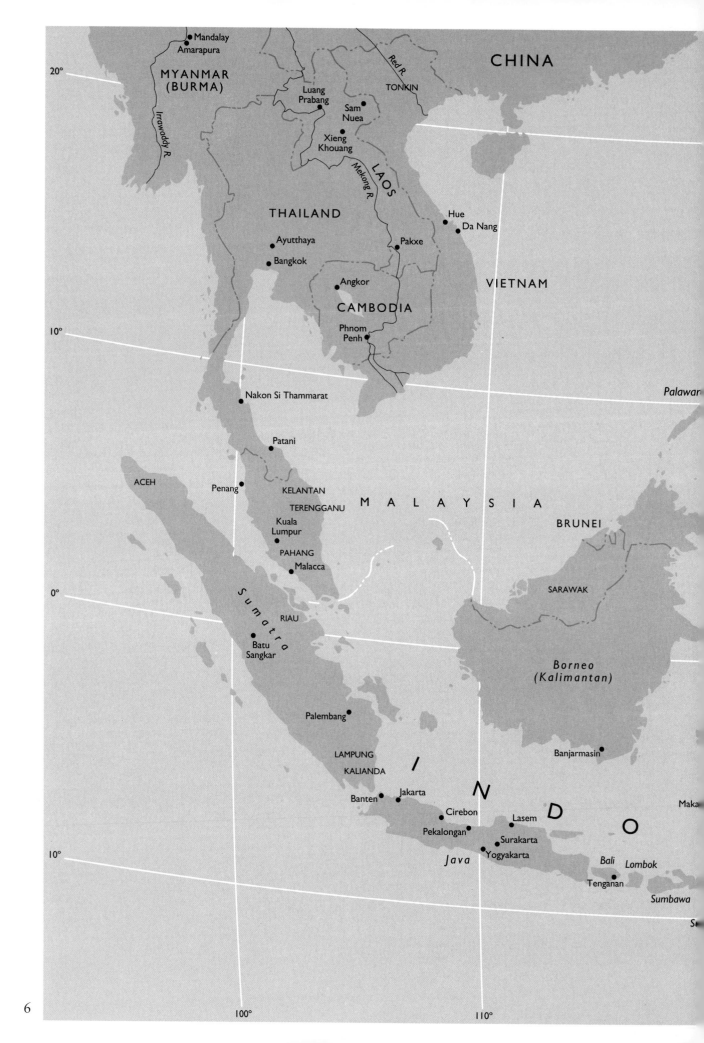

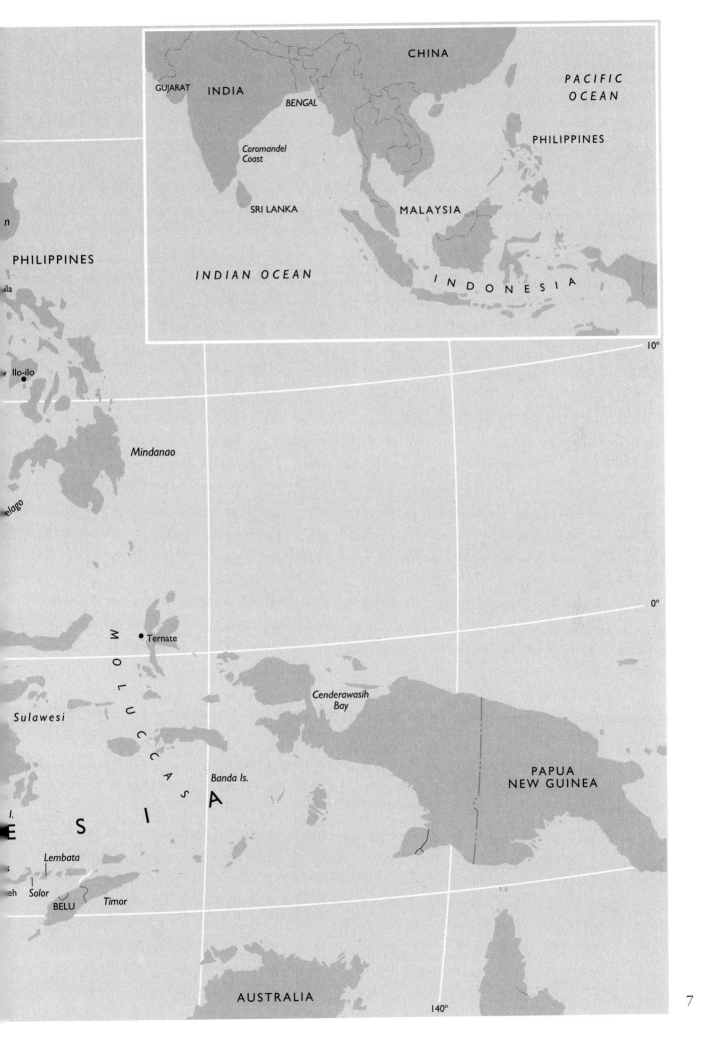

GUJARAT INDIA

BENGAL

CHINA

PACIFIC
OCEAN

Coromandel
Coast

PHILIPPINES

SRI LANKA

MALAYSIA

INDIAN OCEAN

I N D O N E S I A

n

PHILIPPINES

ila

Ilo-ilo

elago

Mindanao

Ternate

Cenderawasih
Bay

M
O
L
U
C
C
A
S

Sulawesi

PAPUA
NEW GUINEA

Banda Is.

E   S   I

Lembata

Solor

BELU   Timor

AUSTRALIA

10°

0°

140°

7

Southeast Asia:
A Region and a Crossroad

ANTHONY REID

The geography of Southeast Asia ensured that it would be a region both distinctive in itself and open to myriad influences from outside. Like the Middle East or the Low Countries, it straddles one of the great passages of the world's trade. Every individual, trade item or idea moving by sea between China and Japan on the one hand and the remainder of the Eurasian civilizations on the other hand had to traverse it. Unlike those other crossroads, however, Southeast Asia was a region of thousands of islands and dozens of mighty rivers. All major population centres were linked by water. The exchange of goods both within and beyond the region was easy and natural, and truly subsistence communities were found, if at all, only among mountain-dwelling minorities. As a French traveller said of eastern Indonesia in about 1600, the separate islands 'abound only in one particular thing ... So this one product ... must furnish them with all else; this is why ... these people are constrained to keep up continual intercourse with one another, the one supplying what the other wants'.[1]

The peoples of the region are so diverse in language, religion and high culture that they might seem to defy categorization. Their languages alone are much more diverse than those of Europe. For most of the last two thousand years the region has been dominated by Austronesian (Malayo-Polynesian) languages in virtually all the islands, the Peninsula and what is now the central Vietnamese coast, and by the very different Mon-Khmer language group in most of the river valleys of the mainland. The southward movement of successful warrior elites subsequently imposed Burmese as the dominant language of the Irrawaddy valley and two tonal language groups, T'ai (embracing Thai, Lao, Shan and many others) and Vietnamese, in the rest of the mainland except modern Cambodia. Yet despite this diversity, Southeast Asian languages share many similar constructions which show the intensity with which they once interacted in the region.

In religion a series of reformist waves between the eleventh and the sixteenth centuries wedded Burma, Siam, Laos and Cambodia firmly to the Theravada school of Sri Lankan Buddhism, whose characteristic feature is the saffron-robed celibate monk. On the other hand, the coastal areas of the Peninsula and the Indonesian Archipelago embraced Islam between about 1300 and 1650, while Catholic Christianity was successfully spread to lowland Filipinos by the Spanish in a few decades between 1570 and 1650. The Vietnamese monarchy established Confucianism as a state orthodoxy in the fifteenth century, and progressively spread it southwards in the subsequent four centuries at the expense of Mahayana Buddhism and animism. Beneath these commitments to separate religious systems, however, Southeast Asians never lost their common older pattern of belief in a world of spirits of the dead, the ritual satisfaction of which was necessary for health and welfare. In the courts there was also an enduring common legacy of Hinduism in state rituals and in the great

1. *The Voyage of Francis Pyrard of Laval to the East Indies, the Maldives, the Moluccas, and Brazil*, trans. A. Gray (London: Hakluyt Society, 1887–89), vol. II, p. 169.

popular epics (the *Ramayana* and the *Mahabharata*).

Many of the features which give Southeast Asia its identity can be attributed to a humid tropical environment, where rainfall is heavy and seasonal, an annual flooding of the rivers relatively predictable, and forest and water the dominant physical features. The forest was generous with building materials for housing — wood and bamboo for the structure and palm-leaf for the roof. Almost everywhere (northern Vietnam, Java, Bali and the Moluccas had become the exceptions by the seventeenth century) domestic houses were raised far above the ground on wooden poles, as a protection from flooding on the plains and from animals and enemies in the forests. Only religious edifices were built of permanent materials. Boats were more common than horses as a means of everyday transport.

The environment must also have determined to some extent the universal diet of rice and fish, but common tastes went much further than that. A paste of half-fermented fish or prawn was everywhere the favoured garnish for rice, and palm-wine and a chewed quid of betel the indispensable narcotics and social stimulants. At festivals for different kings and gods, similar spectacles and entertainments were enjoyed, of which the most characteristic were animal contests (from popular cricket-fights at one extreme to the royal elephant combat at the other), bronze gong orchestras, decorous dances and the kick-volleyball now played at the Southeast Asia Games under its Thai name *takraw*. Southeast Asia as a whole parted company from its giant neighbours, India and China, in the prominence and economic autonomy enjoyed by women, whose functions included planting and harvesting rice as well as marketing. Many foreign traders were surprised to find themselves dealing with women in the market, from a Chinese in thirteenth-century Angkor ('In Cambodia it is the women who take charge of trade') to a British statesman in nineteenth-century Java ('The women alone attend to the markets, and conduct all the business of buying and selling').[2]

Its strategic location and its spices and aromatics brought outsiders to Southeast Asia, but they came predominantly by sea in manageable numbers. Only Vietnam (then limited to the Red River Delta area) was effectively ruled by outsiders before the era of European colonialism. For almost a thousand years before 939 AD, and at some intervals thereafter, Vietnam was a Chinese province, and adopted China's writing system and many of its mores. The fierceness with which Vietnam defended its independence once won, however, effectively closed the only easy land route by which China might have expanded southwards. Because China was little interested in shipping or naval adventure before the southern Sung dynasty (1127–1279), the remainder of Southeast Asia during the first millennium was more exposed to influences from the west, and particularly India. Sanskrit-derived writing systems, a selection of the Vedic gods and epics, and many literary and artistic models found their way 'below the winds' to Southeast Asia along with Indian traders during the first millennium of the Christian era. Nevertheless, the sea journey from South China was the easier one, and once Chinese began making it in significant numbers from the twelfth century onwards, they made a great contribution to Southeast Asian shipbuilding, ceramics, firearms, paper,

2. Paul Pelliot, *Mémoires sur les coutumes du Cambodge de Tcheou Ta-Kouan* (Paris: Adrien Maisonneuve, 1951), p. 20; Thomas Stamford Raffles, *The History of Java*, 2 vols (London: Black, Parbury and Allen, 1817), I: 353.

"The Prince of Madura",
*a hand-coloured lithograph by C.W. Mieling
after a drawing by A. van Pers,
published in Nederlandsch Oost-Indische
Typen, The Hague, Koninklijke Steendrukkerij,
1855
(Australian National Gallery Library
Research Collection).*

coinage, weights, cuisine and material culture in general. By prospering through trade and then intermarrying with the local aristocracy, they also helped create new Southeast Asian elites at a number of different stages from the fifteenth century (notably in Java) to the twentieth century (most successfully in Thailand).

Despite that early period when elements of Indian civilization were adapted into Southeast Asia, caste remained almost unknown (Bali alone acknowledges caste, but in a very attenuated form). Status was (and is) greatly emphasized, and displayed through dress, umbrellas and a numerous retinue of followers. Yet this did not prevent a greater degree of social and geographic mobility than elsewhere in Asia. The records are full of upstart traders, warriors, slaves and foreigners rising in royal service or beginning dynasties of their own. Perhaps it was this very uneasiness about origins which encouraged the display of status markers. A relatively fluid form of slavery was widespread, with many entering that state through warfare, debt or misdemeanour, and leaving it again through diligence or good fortune. The central feature of the social system was the control of manpower, and individuals gained power and status to the extent that they could draw others to their service through debt, obligation or capture. A Chinese reported that sixteenth-century Malays, for example, said that 'it is better to have slaves than to have land, because slaves are a protection to their masters'.[3] Wars were fought predominantly to acquire manpower and often resulted in great movements of peoples.

3. Hwang Chung, in W.P. Groeneveldt (ed.), *Historical Notes on Indonesia and Malaya, Compiled from Chinese Sources* (Batavia, 1880; reprinted Jakarta: Bhratara, 1960), p. 128.

Physical appearance was and is one of the principal means of displaying status. Europeans have often been surprised at how lavish Southeast Asians are with their dress, as opposed to the relative simplicity of their diet and their housing. 'They are not above the vanity of valuing themselves on the smartness of their dress, a failing which often leads them into extravagance. You will often see a well-dressed man without a single *quan* in his possession.'[4] The major item of non-essential expenditure in pre-modern Southeast Asian households was likely to be clothing and jewellery. While the poor and the isolated wove their own cloth, those who could afford them delighted in imported cloths as rare and fine as could be obtained. First Indian and Arab traders, and later Europeans, were able to penetrate the markets of Southeast Asia primarily because they brought the brightly coloured cloths of Coromandel, Gujarat and Bengal to exchange for the spices of the region.

Indian cottons and Chinese silks were probably among the earliest items brought into Southeast Asia to exchange for the spices and forest products of the region. Chinese traders reported on the presence of cotton cloths in the markets of the region from at least the thirteenth century, some of which were produced locally but some undoubtedly imported from India. In the fifteenth century the trade expanded, as the export of pepper and spices westwards picked up in response to rising European and Middle Eastern demand. The growing dimensions of this trade led to a steady increase in the volume of Indian cloth imports, until a peak was reached in the first half of the seventeenth century when about one and a half million pieces of cloth were imported into Southeast Asia from India. On average, these pieces were long enough for several sarongs, so that one may calculate that enough Indian cloth was imported to provide about a quarter of the total population with a new lower garment every year.

An indication of Southeast Asia's dependence on imported cloth at that time is the Dutch factor Stalpaert's survey of the cloth market of Banda, the group of tiny nutmeg-producing islands of eastern Indonesia, in 1603. Of the 61 000 pieces of cloth imported each year (presumably largely for re-export), 88 per cent was from India as against only 12 per cent of Southeast Asian cloth, divided in its origin between the cotton-growing regions of Sumbawa and Bali.[5]

This was the peak pre-modern period of commercial prosperity for Southeast Asians. Between about 1590 and 1640 the whole world appeared to be competing to buy the clove and nutmeg of the Moluccas, the pepper of Sumatra and the Peninsula, the sandalwood of Timor, and the sappanwood, deerhides, benzoin, camphor and lacquer of the Mainland states. The Dutch, English and other Europeans broke the Portuguese monopoly around the Cape of Good Hope; the Japanese broke briefly out of their isolation to carry their silver in vast quantities to the south; and China also experienced one of its periods of relative freedom of overseas trade. New entrepots sprang up to cater for this demand. Many of them, such as Aceh, Palembang, Banten, Makassar, Patani, Ternate (the clove centre) and the Vietnamese port of Hoi An (near modern Danang), created or sustained new states which reached their peak of power and affluence in the first half of the seventeenth century. The influx of trade wealth and of European

4. George Finlayson,
The Mission to Siam and Hué, 1821–1822
(London: John Murray, 1826; reprinted
Singapore: Oxford University Press, 1988),
p. 378.

A nineteenth-century black-and-white illustration of Burmese cloth-sellers in Laos.

5. Stalpaert's memorandum is reproduced in
G.P. Rouffaer, *Die Indische Batikkunst und Ihre Geschichte*, (1899).

and Chinese firearms enabled these and other states to dominate their hinterlands as never before, to build impressive cities and fleets, and to hold their own against the troublesome Europeans.

This commercial age not only brought Indian textiles, Chinese ceramics and European arms to the region. It also created the conditions for a transformation of its religious systems. Although the leading courts had adapted Hindu and Buddhist ideas from India centuries earlier, the dominant popular religious system was a type of animism based on the need to placate the spirits of the dead by ritual and sacrificial means. The commercial orientation of the period from 1400 to 1650, however, created on the one hand a cosmopolitan trading class committed to Islam or one of the other universal religions, and on the other hand centralizing kings who found that the scriptural religions provided a means of breaking with a past of political fragmentation. By 1650 most of the Archipelago was officially Muslim, the lowland Philippines Catholic, and Burma and Siam committed to the Mahavihara reformist order of Sri Lankan Buddhism.

This rapid spread of new ideas and foreign goods brought profound changes in clothing styles. Before 1500 sewn garments were rare, and most Southeast Asians wore only a wrap-around lower garment, with the upper body clothed, if at all, by a loose scarf or breast-cloth. Only the Vietnamese were, by European or Chinese standards, 'fully dressed'. The new faiths demanded greater modesty and discouraged decoration of the body itself as a work of supernatural art. Hence tattooing, distended ear-lobes, long male hair, long fingernails and penis implants all disappeared or retreated to the hills. At the same time the flood of imported cloth provided opportunities for experimentation. Sarongs descended below the knees, and sewn upper garments became widespread for both women and men. Filipinos quickly adopted a modified Spanish style of dress. The 'traditional' dress of Southeast Asia basically dates from this period, though modified and formalized again under colonial influence in the late nineteenth century.

The openness of Southeast Asia to waterborne shipping was not always an advantage. The eager competition of the sixteenth century was gradually replaced in the seventeenth century by a monopoly in the hands of the most successful capitalist institution of its day — the Dutch East India Company (VOC). By the 1620s it had 150 ships at its disposal in Asian waters, and in the 1660s over 250. These were the principal weapons of a concerted strategy to monopolize key items of the trade of Asia. From its Asian headquarters in Batavia (Jakarta), the VOC struck first at the most vulnerable items of international trade concentrated on certain small islands. The world's supply of nutmeg was in its hands when it conquered and depopulated Banda in 1621, while the cloves of the Moluccas and the cinnamon of Sri Lanka were effectively Dutch by the end of the struggles of the 1650s. Pepper had to be shared with the English Company and Chinese shippers, but the VOC imposed a local buying monopoly by force at many of the crucial markets. The Company also attempted to take over the supply of Indian textiles to Southeast Asia, though it succeeded in excluding the Indian suppliers only where it had local control of the seas, as in the Moluccas, Java and southern Sumatra.

VOC domination of the most lucrative arteries of trade, accompanied by its physical conquest of port-cities such as Jakarta (1619), Malacca (1641), Palembang (1659), Makassar (1669) and Banten (1682), turned Southeast Asians away from dependence on international commerce for their livelihood. The prices paid to growers for their produce dropped, the prices of VOC-controlled Indian cloth rose, while the threat of a Dutch naval blockade discouraged reliance on the international market for vital supplies. There was in the second half of the seventeenth century a move to greater self-sufficiency, while once-great cities lost much of their raison d'être. Two commercially oriented peoples, the coastal Javanese and the Mons of southern Burma, were squeezed out of maritime trade altogether by the twin pressures of Europeans by sea and interior rivals by land.

This trend provided an opportunity for local producers, who could weave cloth more cheaply and evade the Dutch monopoly. In the late seventeenth century Java emerged for the first time as a significant exporter of cloth to other islands. 'The Javanese, having become poor and indigent ... have been forced to resort, more than they otherwise would, to weaving their cloths themselves, not only for their own use but also to sell to those in other places.'[6] In South Sumatra and southern Borneo cheaper Javanese luriks and batiks began to displace the more brightly coloured Indian cloths supplied by the VOC, while locals also defied Dutch bans by growing cotton and weaving cloth at home. The royal chronicle of Banjar, a southern Borneo kingdom, made a virtue of the trend by stressing that the flamboyant borrowing of an earlier period had brought ruin on the country: 'Do not any of you dress according to the style of the Dutch, or of the Chinese, or of the Siamese, or of the Acehnese, or of the Makassarese, or of the Bugis ...We should all dress like the Javanese'.[7]

Probably the largest export centre of eighteenth-century Southeast Asia developed in South Sulawesi, on the small island of Salayer and the adjacent coast. Their long dry season allowed cotton to flourish where rice did not. Salayer checked cottons were being traded as far as Manila and Borneo in the late seventeenth century, and all over the Malay world in the eighteenth century. In the Philippines a major centre of cotton-growing developed on the island of Panay, where the weavers of Ilo-ilo provided cloth for much of the Spanish colony. Cotton was also grown on a large scale in eastern Java, Bali, Sumbawa, on the mainland on the west bank of the Mekong above Phnom Penh and in central Burma. Only in Vietnam was silk more important for clothing, though silkworms were also grown to produce a high-grade cloth in Aceh (northern Sumatra) and South Sulawesi, and imported silk was woven in central Burma and many other centres.

Though these were specialized export centres, cotton was grown very widely, probably representing the second most valuable crop after rice until the rise of colonial sugar estates in the nineteenth century. In the urban centres the spinning wheel had made its entry by the sixteenth century, though the drop-spindle remained common in rural areas. The women of almost every region wove their own cloth in a great variety of styles. Women used a narrow backstrap loom to make their cloth. The larger, more efficient wooden looms of India, China or

6. 'General letter' of 1684, in *Generale Missieven van Gouverneurs-Generaal en Raden aan Heren XVII der Verenigde Oostindische Compagnie*, ed. W.Ph. Coolhaas, vol. IV (The Hague: Martinus Nijhoff, 1971), p. 673.

7. J.J. Ras (ed.), *Hikajat Bandjar: A Study in Malay Historiography* (The Hague: Martinus Nijhoff, 1968), p. 264; see also pp. 330, 336.

Europe did not spread to Southeast Asia until the twentieth century, so that production remained slow and the cloths narrow.

In the eighteenth century the Dutch and English Companies replaced Indian cloth with opium as the preferred trade item for Southeast Asia, to exchange for its pepper, forest products and now also coffee, sugar and gambir. Opium was compact and convenient, easy to monopolize at source in Bengal, had a huge profit margin, and held its market even when consumers' living standards dropped. Nevertheless, the Companies atrophied and grew monstrously inefficient through corruption and political involvements. This created space for new forces to stir in the region. Chinese migrants opened new commercial frontiers in the Gulf of Thailand, in the Malayan Peninsula (mining tin and growing gambir), and in the gold mines of western Borneo. Private Asia-based English and French traders and after 1776 New Englanders, as well as South Indian Muslims and southern Chinese, undercut the Companies by paying commercial prices. Within the region, Bugis from Sulawesi (Celebes) were the most successful in establishing trading networks throughout the Archipelago, rivalling the Chinese boat-owners who also collected produce for sale in the major ports.

Was it this freeing-up of commercial opportunities, or perhaps the greater internal strength of regimes which had learned to do without foreign commerce, which breathed some new life into Southeast Asian states in the late eighteenth and early nineteenth centuries? One cannot deny such life when contemplating the temple murals which decorated the new Thai capital built first at Thonburi, and later across the river at Bangkok, on the ruins of the Burmese destruction of Ayutthaya in 1767; nor the magnificent palaces and illustrated manuscripts which the Konbaung dynasty (1752–1885) produced in its capitals near modern Mandalay in Burma; nor the charm of the capital built at Hue by the Nguyen Dynasty which reunified Vietnam. Even in the islands, where the Dutch and Spanish had established their respective spheres of domination, a modicum of peace and prosperity in this period enabled the kingdoms of Yogyakarta, Surakarta, Aceh, Palembang, Riau, Terengganu, Lombok and Sulu to show a coherence and vigour which are still evident in their surviving literature.

This was not enough, however, to prevent all these states from being seen as anachronistic impediments to commerce by the rising industrial powers of Europe. Most of the stronger states were brought down by bitter wars which destroyed their dynasties and incorporated them into 'modern' colonies. Burma was conquered in three bites by Britain —1824–6, 1852–3 and 1885; Vietnam in two bites by France — 1858–62 and 1882–5. The machine-gun, the steamship and British acquiescence enabled Spain and Holland to round out their empires with a series of conquests, notably of Aceh (1873–1903), Lombok (1894), the Bugis states (1905–6), Bali (1906–8) and Sulu (1879). Other kingdoms bent before the wind by accepting European advisers, with Thailand the most successful in reconciling this path with a universally recognized sovereignty.

The true colonial era spanning the years from about 1880 to 1942 was one of extraordinary transformation, in which Southeast Asians

An 1865 photograph by van Kinsberger of Gusti Ketut Jelantik, Raja of Buleleng in north Bali, with his scribe.

were forced to join the modern European-dominated world whether they liked it or not. Colonial estate agriculture and modern transport networks caused exports to boom, court-centred polities were replaced by bureaucratically governed territorial units, and new elites were created by the beginnings of Western-style education. Despite these changes, however, the majority of Southeast Asia's people were separated further than ever from the dynamic factors of change by a layered 'plural society', in which Europeans (and a few 'protected' rulers) held all the reins of power, while Chinese and Indians occupied most of the entrepreneurial and skilled roles in the economy. The majority of the population increased unprecedentedly in numbers as a result of the colonial peace, but became 'peasantized' in low-productivity agriculture, largely of subsistence food crops. Average living standards failed to rise at all during the colonial era, with the possible exception of the American Philippines.

Textiles illustrate the problem well. In the eighteenth century Southeast Asians produced their own cloth for the most part, with some coarse cottons still being imported from southeastern India at the bottom of the market, and Gujarati silk *patola* at the top. British machine-made cloth could in the nineteenth century outsell the labour-intensive local product in both price and fineness, however. Lancashire cottons began to make inroads in Sumatra and Malaya in the early 1800s, and virtually took over Java during the period the British administered the island (1811–16). From the British ports of Penang and Singapore cloth manufactured according to local tastes spread throughout the region in the 1820s and 1830s. The Philippine market was somewhat protected by distance and Spanish policy, and the Ilo-ilo production of pineapple-fibre as well as cotton cloth did not yield until the 1860s, when its 60 000 looms were vanquished in just a few years. Rather than modernize the indigenous textile industries to survive this challenge, the French and Dutch colonial governments seized the opportunity of a privileged outlet for their own struggling textile industries at home. Southeast Asian production of exquisite cloths by hand survived only in remote uplands and islands where the imports could not reach, or as expensive luxuries for the courts and for foreign collectors.

In one sense the colonial era ended abruptly with the Japanese invasion exactly fifty years ago, since the European regimes were never able to establish themselves with the same authority after the war. In another sense the region entered a profound crisis which might be considered to have lasted from the depression of the 1930s (from which some of the colonial agricultural exports never recovered) to the reunification of Vietnam in 1975 (though for Cambodia and Burma the crisis is not over yet). Nationalism was the path chosen by all the elites of the region (however elaborated with Marxist or religious rhetoric) to escape the deep humiliation of colonialism, and to restore control of their own destinies. This path carried a heavy price in economic chaos and political violence, however, especially for Indonesia, the Indo-China countries and Burma, which pursued it through revolution, war, external intervention and internal repression.

Though they rejected Western political and economic domination, the nationalists greatly accelerated the process of cultural change, whereby the cigarette replaced the betel quid, trousers the sarong, and roman scripts the older Indic, Chinese or Arabic-based ones. In the name of modernization and national equality Western modes of thought and dress became more popular than ever.

The last two decades have begun at last to bring the rewards of that crisis of re-established sovereignty, not only for the elites but also for the great mass of the population. Education has become nearly universal, child mortality is dropping and life expectancy rising rapidly, and real per capita income levels in Thailand, Malaysia, Singapore and Indonesia are rising as rapidly as anywhere in the world.

Once again the textile industry illustrates the trend. Very modest beginnings were made in the direction of mechanized spinning and weaving in the early years of the century, particularly in Tonkin (northern Vietnam) and Java. These were much extended in the 1930s, as an import substitution measure in the Depression years. Nevertheless, all Southeast Asian countries remained importers of textiles on a grand scale until the 1960s, when local production expanded quickly. In the 1980s Southeast Asia became for the first time in its history a net exporter of textiles, and this industry is playing a major part in a manufacturing revolution currently under way. Like Japan and Korea before them, Southeast Asian countries are now undergoing at an extraordinary rate the exciting and often profoundly disturbing transformation which we know as industrialization.

An Indonesian mosque with a tiered-roof typical of earlier Hindu architecture.

Traditions Transformed:
The Cultural Context of Textile Making and Use in Southeast Asia

ROBYN MAXWELL

The arts of Southeast Asia are remarkable for their rich diversity: powerful wooden ancestral figures, Hindu heroes in stone, ornate gilt images of the Lord Buddha, puppet characters formed from Arabic calligraphy, and statues of the Madonna and Child have been created by the artisans of this fascinating region. In no art form is this variety so apparent and are the permutations so numerous as in the region's textiles.[1]

The great diversity found among the textiles of Southeast Asia can be explained partly in terms of varying geographic locations, political entities, economic bases and historical circumstances. It can also be attributed to the vigorous creativity of local textile makers. However, shared experiences — of religions, social and political structures, languages, technologies and trade — are also readily apparent in the region's artistic traditions. The common and central importance of textiles in the lives of Southeast Asian peoples invites a more systematic analysis of regional responses to such stimuli.

The textile traditions of Southeast Asia stretch back into prehistory. The first fabrics were no doubt made by means of interlacing and knotting techniques at which Southeast Asians are still very adept. Building materials, mats, containers and apparel constructed of plaited vegetable fibres are features of rural and urban life. Until recent changes in the political systems of rural parts of the region, spectacular jackets and tabards were important items of apparel for warriors — protective in inter-village battles and prominent in the many rites which surrounded the ancestral customs of warfare and head-hunting.

Many basketry items are interwoven with schematic and figurative designs, often in the oldest colour combinations of the region — black, red and white. The survival of this primordial tricolour in the face of the rainbow palette of modern synthetic dyes attests to the strength of continuing Southeast Asian aesthetics, and to the symbolic importance that blue-black, red and white have assumed.

The discoveries, in numerous archaeological sites in insular and mainland Southeast Asia, of stone bark-beaters similar to those still used in remote pockets of the region to produce soft felted fabrics attest to the antiquity of this textile process. Used for everyday and ritual garments in village society today, bark-cloth is often decorated with pigments. In the past fine bark-cloth provided the foundation for the pigment and ink paintings of the great Javanese and Balinese courts.

Like matting and woven fabric, bark-cloth is sometimes embellished with bright attractive substances — seed, beads, mica and shells. Archaeological finds suggest that this form of supplementary ornamentation has also been applied since antiquity. In some parts of the region, however, the appliqué of precious objects onto base materials

1. A full account of the historical development of the textile traditions of Southeast Asia, their role and the meaning of cloth in everyday and ceremonial life, as well as the impact of foreign influences on these traditions, can be found in my book, *Textiles of Southeast Asia: Tradition, Trade and Transformation*, co-published by the Australian National Gallery and Oxford University Press, Melbourne, 1990.

provides the main means of artistic expression on textiles required for ceremonial use, and the entire surface of garments is covered, for example, with complex beaded designs. The rarity of these materials — acquired through adventure and trade — adds to the value and ritual significance of the garment on which they appear.

Simple weaving apparatus, such as the foot-braced backstrap loom, identifiable on finds of prehistoric bronze, continue to be used for the production of cotton textiles in Cambodia and southern Laos. In fact, the backstrap tension loom so widely found throughout the islands of Indonesia and the Philippines suggests that this technology has been used in the region, with only minor developments, for at least three thousand years. The vegetable fibres woven on these looms have changed over time, with cotton replacing hemp, banana and pineapple fibres, and thread made from leaves and palm fronds, in all but a few isolated locations.

However, whether with the crisp fibres of the swamp grass, *Curculigo latifolia*, or with locally grown and handspun cotton thread, the means of ornamenting woven vegetable fibre show great similarity across Southeast Asia. And the motifs and patterns achieved from bold warp stripes, the ikat resist-tying of warp threads and supplementary weft wrapping and weaving techniques often reveal similar sources of inspiration. In particular, the physical and spiritual worlds are sources of motifs for weavers, although these are often difficult to discern amid the intricate arrangements of spirals, hooks, diamonds and dots which characterize the region's textile designs.

The ship, a potent symbol of transition at various stages in the life cycle, also appears to have been an early motif in Southeast Asian art. It has remained an important image on the textiles of the region, demonstrating the permanence of meaningful symbols, and the variations which time and technological, cultural and aesthetic changes have wrought. Thus we find examples of Southeast Asian textiles made about the same period which feature basic canoes, multi-masted galleons, dragon boats with serpent prows, local trading *prahu* and modern steamers.

Clothing is one of the oldest functions of the textiles, and the shape of a garment, its colour, design and motif indicate important and fundamental information about the wearer. Gender, age, marital status, clan membership, and district or village origins may be read from a particular textile or the way in which it is worn. The more powerful and often the most elaborate textiles are reserved for those of considerable social and ritual maturity — the elders, the warriors, the religious specialists. Many older types of textile were specifically associated with events related to the origins of the clan or village, the ancestral deities and local spirits, and the general well-being of the social unit. Some textile forms, such as the long narrow loin-cloth, have been adapted from man's apparel to ceremonial banners and hangings.

One of the most important developments in Southeast Asian textile history was the spread of sericulture and the importation of silk thread into Southeast Asia in early historical times. One early change to the region's backstrap loom must have been the introduction of the reed or comb, a modification which enabled the easier handling of the

A turn-of-the-century photograph by the anthropologist F. Cooper-Cole of a group of Batak people dressed in painted bark-cloth for a wedding ceremony on the island of Palawan in the central Philippines.

finer silk threads. Throughout the mainland, another, probably later, development was the incorporation of treadle-operated heddles. In some places an Indian-style spinning wheel replaced the older drop-weight spindle for spinning and winding thread.

With the introduction of silk and the reed came a new range of textile types — decorated with weft rather than the older warp techniques. Weft ikat, supplementary weft brocades and weft banding are prominent features of the silk textiles of the Southeast Asian region.

Since the growth of silk technology coincided with the spread of Indian religions and the rise of political states within the region, it is not surprising that the luxury textiles created from silks and gold threads became synonymous with the nascent Indic courts of Southeast Asia. Apart from fine apparel — sumptuous skirtcloths held in place by and complemented with exquisite jewellery — this high rank was manifested in the public display of opulent fabrics by the rulers and their nobility, including parasols and canopies of state, rich furnishings and glittering regalia, and in the bestowal of special textiles as gifts to loyal followers. The gender distinctions still obvious in village clothing throughout the region diminished in favour of richly decorated court textiles which displayed the relative status of courtiers through careful gradations of colour, intricacies of central design and

The costumes of these members of a Burmese theatre troupe show the tapestry weave silks and heavily embroidered aprons and collars of the court.

border patterns, and size. Exclusive rights to wear certain motifs and textiles were awarded to certain officials and their families.

The place of textiles in ceremonial exchange is clearly of ancient origin, binding families and clans in close and continuing alliances. Even today, special types of cloth are given on such occasions as childbirth, attainment of adulthood, marriage and death, as well as on other appropriate occasions in the life cycle. These occasions, of course, vary from one society to another, with adulthood, for instance, achieved by tattooing or tooth-filing, hair-cutting or circumcision, marriage or teenage segregation. In Southeast Asia, all such events require the presence of fine textiles, and are often the occasion for conspicuous presentations.

The chronicles of Southeast Asia record that princes were magnanimous in their generosity to their sovereigns and to their followers. The textile gifts they gave were precious and highly valued. Textiles produced in silk and gold thread, however, had little of the magic and mystery of their more ancient vegetable fibre counterparts. The rituals that surround the application of special dyes, the setting up of the loom, the severing of the continuous warp and the protective and magical functions of the resulting cloth are generally absent in sericulture. The silks are instead symbols of high status: their size, colour, the intricacy of design and the exclusivity of pattern draw attention to the rank of the wearer and his or her relationship to the centre and source of power. As in the past, prestige textiles continue to be embellished with significant, often valuable objects, which add to their beauty and consequence. Gold and silver ribbon, mica, sequins, mirror pieces and coins are sometimes incorporated into the surface decoration of textiles required for ceremonial use.

Alongside fine locally made textiles, exotic imported fabrics have also been highly esteemed. Travellers and shipping documents record a vigorous trade in a wide range of textiles, especially luxury items ranging in time and place from Chinese silks, and Persian brocades, to Turkish embroideries and European flannel. Of by far the most lasting importance was the trade in Indian textiles. The fine silk double ikat *patola* and the brightly painted and block-printed mordant-dyed cottons not only were much desired trade commodities throughout Southeast Asia, but remained valuable long after trade links had been severed.

Today, two centuries after the demise of the great European trading companies, Indian *patola* and mordant-dyed cottons are prized possessions, symbols of power and sacred heirlooms in insular and mainland Southeast Asia. The impact of Indian cloths on motifs and the design structure of the region's textiles has been enormous, as Southeast Asian craftswomen, fascinated by their potency and inspired by their beauty, have recreated textiles in the image of their family or village treasures.

The range of designs found on Indian trade textiles documents the extent of international commerce at its height in the seventeenth and early eighteenth centuries. Indian cloth in Southeast Asian treasuries may display Indian classical styles, Persian designs, European motifs, or patterns specifically intended for a regional market. The intricate mordant-painted cottons created for the central Thai kingdoms, for example, were filled with motifs and ornamentation in distinct design formats, peculiar to Thai tastes of the time. On the other hand, for eastern Indonesian destinations, small border designs of elephants for Indian saris were magnified into impressive motifs for hangings.

As textiles play such an important role in the region's ritual life, changes in religious ideas and symbols have, over time, had considerable impact on the range of motifs and patterns applied to textiles. The traditional arts have been evolving for millennia, with new images being incorporated, sometimes at the expense of older forms, sometimes intertwined with and alongside ancient designs. Hindu shrines in Bali still require special hangings, no longer found in

The ceremonial dress of the Thai court incorporated many influences — Indian, Chinese and European — into a distinctive Thai style.

neighbouring Indonesian cultures where Islam is now dominant, yet bearing considerable resemblance to the prayer flags of Thailand and Laos.

From the earliest times, the arts of Southeast Asia have displayed both schematic and figurative designs, and these have continued to be evident on textiles of the region to the present time. The meanings of many of the most ancient motifs, however, may have been lost in the distant past, or only a century or two ago, while the significance of others has disappeared in the rapidly changing environments of the late colonial and post-independence eras of this century.

Many popular figurative images, however, are still easily recognizable. Scenes from the classical epics of India — the *Ramayana*, the *Mahabharata* and *Jataka* tales of the life of the Lord Buddha — can be identified on textiles across the Southeast Asian region. Such legendary figures and scenes are particularly evident on textiles intended for religious use. While the images would rarely be placed on garments to be worn around the lower body, they abound on ceremonial hangings and Buddhist offerings of merit.

The introduction of another great world religion, Islam, into much of the region has of course also led to changes in existing designs. The Malay communities of the Malay peninsula, Sumatra and Borneo have largely moved away from the depiction of legendary figures in favour of floral and arabesque patterns, although the Prophet's mount, the winged *bouraq*, is a popular motif on ceremonial hangings. Other creatures such as birds and lions can often be distinguished on the spectacular calligraphic batik cloths used by Islamic communities in Sumatra and Java as shrouds, hangings, headcloths and shawls.

While over centuries Chinese traders played a prominent role in supplying much-desired silk thread and textiles, relatively few fine Chinese fabrics survive to demonstrate the types favoured by Southeast Asians, although these were also apparently in great demand in the courts of the region. In the nineteenth century, however, the ruling chiefs of Mindanao wore fabulous jackets embroidered with huge dragons, while in the courts of Laos, princesses donned skirts and stoles of rich Chinese brocades trimmed with gold-thread embroidery.

Although, like many textile traditions of Southeast Asia, the gold-thread hangings and accessories prominent at weddings and other celebrations are the result of the confluence of many external influences — Indian, Central Asian and European — the Chinese contribution is particularly obvious. In fact, embroidered objects, incorporating gold thread, minuscule beads and rainbow-coloured silk, became the hallmark of the textile traditions of mestizo Chinese communities of the Malay peninsula and Sumatra. The textiles of these Baba groups, who are the result of intermarriage between local Malay women and Chinese immigrants, are a quirky combination of the features of both heritages — Chinese cloud-collars are paired with Malay ornamental kerchiefs, imperial gowns are worn for weddings, and batik skirt-cloths for everyday dress.

The development of the well-known Javanese batik, probably in the sixteenth and seventeenth centuries in direct response to and strong competition with the Indian trade cottons, provided a fluid medium for new designs. Less constrained by repetition than the weaver, the batik maker used her pen-like *canting* to wax a wide range of designs, figurative and geometric. These designs reflected the tastes of both the communities which made them and those with which they were traded. The brightly coloured floral patterns, so popular among the immigrant Chinese groups of the region, have influenced modern printed cloth in every nation of Southeast Asia. Thus the delicate and intricately hand-worked cloth of the urban elites of Java, Singapore and the Malay peninsula in the nineteenth century provided the model for the cheapest skirtcloth materials for many of the poorest women of the region today.

Like the Indian, Arab and Chinese traders, Europeans in Southeast Asia also intermarried with local women. The resulting mestizo Indo-European culture also contributed to the changing textile traditions of the region. In particular, a move towards greater realism in the depiction of motifs was one characteristic of textile designs where European influence is significant. Often this involved the replacement of schematic floral patterns with discernibly European foliage such as roses, irises and bluebells arranged in formal bouquets, around which non-indigenous birds flutter.

Mythical creatures such as angels and cupids became popular on garments — skirtcloths and shawls — for secular wear. Motifs unencumbered by links to ancestral relationships and ceremonial practice became particularly popular in Southeast Asia after World War II, especially for wear by young women. The designs permitted them to display the technical proficiency still so admired, and they stand outside the older social ordering of society. Less lofty, though no less renowned, figures such as the European Red Riding Hood appeared on batik cloth.

While some ancient customs, such as betel-nut chewing, continued into the twentieth century, changes in religious beliefs also brought new customs which required different or modified textile forms. In particular, the conversion to Islam and Christianity encouraged different conceptions of modesty. A woman's upper body, previously wrapped only in a breastcloth for court or temple attendance, was covered with new garments. Tailored shirts, tunics and blouses became more widely used, a trend which has increased with the spread of modern Western attitudes and education throughout most of the region.

Although upper garments are now also worn by men, it is their square headcloth that has become a distinctive feature of the region's dress. Made from a wide range of fabrics — for everyday and formal wear — and tied in an amazing variety of ways, the headcloth, like other traditional textiles, displays many of their fundamental complexities. Sometimes tied to indicate the wearer's rank and occupation, region, village or family of origin, in forms appropriate to the age and ritual maturity of the wearer, the headcloth is also a means of displaying individual creativity and personal style. Young village men and elderly courtiers spend hours developing arrangements which are their individual trademark, and which carry cavalier and romantic titles.

The textiles of Southeast Asia reveal much about their wearers, about their position in society and about the history of that society. Each group makes a range of textiles which is at once distinct, yet linked into a network of other textile traditions. Such traditions are the result of millennia of continuities and changes, of interactions with exotic foreign ideas and objects, and with the familiar and neighbourly. Fashion and individual creativity are valued differently across the region, and at different times. During periods of rapid change, some groups look to the future, while others are wistful about past golden eras. The interplay between the conservation of ancient traditions and the incorporation of challenging and attractive innovations has resulted in an amazing range and variety of textile forms and functions across the Southeast Asian region. It is thus possible to study the textiles of Southeast Asia from a variety of perspectives — looking for continuities or changes, comparing common responses to external stimuli, or studying the myriad differences that have resulted. The richness and the beauty of Southeast Asia's many textile traditions invite and deserve all these responses.

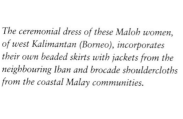

The ceremonial dress of these Maloh women, of west Kalimantan (Borneo), incorporates their own beaded skirts with jackets from the neighbouring Iban and brocade shouldercloths from the coastal Malay communities.

Catalogue

PREPARED AND WRITTEN BY ROBYN MAXWELL

The exhibition objects have been chosen and arranged to illustrate major influences on the textile traditions of Southeast Asia and to show the variety of regional responses to these influences. Each catalogue entry provides the following information: an English explanation of the function of the textile and its local term; the ethnic group, geographic origin and approximate date of the object; the material from which it is made; the decorative techniques used; the measurements (height by width); and the accession number of the object in the collection of the Australian National Gallery.

Early Southeast Asian Textiles:
Materials, Designs and Social Context

There is still considerable evidence, in every country in Southeast Asia, of what the region's earliest textile types must have been. An ancient fabric — felted bark-cloth — is still made in isolated villages with implements similar to those discovered from the distant past. In the twentieth century, bark-cloth is used for clothing: plain for everyday wear but sometimes richly painted with pigments for ceremonial dress. Interlaced matting probably preceded loom-woven fabrics, and mats and basketry still display designs similar to those of woven textiles. The ornamentation of such textiles and matting with beads, shells, seeds and mica has clearly been practised for a very long time.

Woven textiles, however, are also of ancient origin in Southeast Asia. Made on simple looms, they have employed a wide variety of vegetable fibres, including hemp, wild banana thread, fibres from the indigenous pineapple plant, and the leaves and fronds of various other plants and palms, all of which are still used in the region in the twentieth century. Dried and shredded strands of leaves and stalks are knotted and twisted together to form threads sufficiently long for weaving. Over many centuries these vegetable fibres were largely replaced by the more supple cotton thread, locally grown and spun on a drop spindle.

Throughout the region it is largely textiles made from these vegetable fibres that are decorated by the warp ikat process. Bundles of the warp threads intended for the loom are tightly bound (with fibre bindings which resist the introduction of the dyes) into intricate designs before being dyed. The designs appear against the darker, dyed ground when the bindings are cut away.

These and other textiles decorated with warp-oriented techniques such as supplementary weft wrapping and supplementary warp weaving, always interspersed with warp stripes, are still created on backstrap tension looms. Some of these loom types, found in parts of Laos and Cambodia, vary little from the most ancient foot-braced tension looms displayed on the ancient bronze vessels discovered in Yunnan in southern China. Those on which Hmong women of Laos, Thailand and Burma weave narrow strips of hemp fabric incorporate simple treadle-operated heddles.

Many designs found on the textiles of the region have also been part of its artistic repertoire for millennia. Elaborate spirals, circles, triangles, hooked lozenges and arrowhead motifs have been combined to form overall patterns, isolated bands or recognizable forms. Ancient reptilian, bird and human forms can be seen in the ikat and supplementary thread textiles across the length and breadth of Southeast Asia. Even when these are not readily deciphered, the patterns may be identified by their makers in terms of real or mythological creatures which are active participants in that society's social and ritual life. For example, scenarios from dreams are described in the ceremonial cloths of Iban weavers — the most ritually powerful women carefully tying ancestral deities and powerful spirits into their warp ikat and supplementary weft-wrapped designs.

Many textiles are, of course, intended as clothing for ceremonial and everyday wear. The shape and form, the arrangement of designs, the colours and the choice of patterns provide a wealth of information about the wearer. In eastern Indonesia, for instance, cylindrical cloths are worn by women, rectangular forms by men; red-brown is often reserved for ceremony, for the older and ritually mature members of the community, in contrast to indigo-blue for everyday. Bands of design may reveal the clan, village, moiety or rank to which the person belongs.

While textiles appear at most events in the cycle of family and district ceremonies, it is at funerals that they are often most conspicuous in the oldest religious and social structures. Elders and those of greatest prestige may be laid in state under a canopy of fine fabric, or buried with large numbers of the grandest cloths; guests at the mortuary ceremonies will be housed in structures bedecked with huge hangings; families will exchange significant gifts, among which textiles will feature prominently; and spirits in the afterworld will recognize and give safe passage to the deceased on the basis of their burial garments. At all rites the objects used in one of the region's most ancient customs —betel-nut chewing—are wrapped in beautiful containers and textiles.

Two Dawan or Atoni leaders in the ceremonial exchange of betel-nut, in Timor, Indonesia.

1.

2.

1. Mat
Ot Danum people, central Kalimantan,
Indonesia, 19th century
Rattan, natural dyes
Interlacing
112.0 x 181.0 cm
Australian National Gallery 1985.1741

2. Man's headcloth *(siga)*
To Bada people, Bada district, Sulawesi,
Indonesia, early 20th century
Bark-cloth, pigments
Painting
92.0 x 91.0 cm
Australian National Gallery 1982.2296

3. (detail) Ceremonial loincloth and banner
(pio uki')
Kalumpang or Sa'dan Toraja people,
central Sulawesi, Indonesia, early 20th century
Handspun cotton, natural dyes
Supplementary weft weave
517.0 x 51.0 cm
Australian National Gallery 1981.1127

3.

4. Warrior's jacket
Ifugao people, Luzon, Philippines, early 20th century
Bangi *(Caryota cuminggi)* and other fibres, natural dyes
Twining, knotting
85.0 x 72.0 cm
Australian National Gallery 1984.1234

5. (detail) Funeral cloth *(pha vien rong)*
Red T'ai people, Hua Phan province, Laos, 19th century
Handspun cotton, natural dyes
Supplementary weft weave
440.0 x 22.5 cm
Australian National Gallery 1991.1091

4.

5.

6.

6. (detail) Funeral cloth *(pha vien rong)*
T'ai Dam people, Ban Kuay Heup,
Muang Kham, Vietnam, early 20th century
Handspun cotton, silk, natural dyes
Damask weave
768.0 x 61.0 cm
Australian National Gallery 1991.532

7. Woman's jacket and skirt,
(sapé manik and *kain manik)*
Maloh people, Kalimantan, Indonesia,
early 20th century
Beads, shells, sequins, cotton
Bead-work, appliqué
48.5 x 41.5 cm; 58.0 x 42.0 cm
Australian National Gallery 1985.1694a-b

7.

8. Woman's dance apron
Doreri district, Kepala Burung (Bird's Head)
and Cenderawasih Bay region, Irian Jaya,
Indonesia, early 20th century
Beads, fibre thread, commercial cotton cloth
Beading
52.0 x 58.0 cm
Australian National Gallery 1986.2456

9. Cosmetic container and belt
Maranao people, Mindanao, Philippines,
20th century
Beads, buffalo-horn, cotton, wood
Beading, carving
6.6 x 57.0 cm
Australian National Gallery 1986.2117

8.

9.

10.

10. Lidded box for betel-nut ingredients
Paminggir people, Lampung, southern Sumatra,
Indonesia, 19th century
Matting, beads, fibre
Interlacing, bead appliqué
14.0 x 22.0 x 18.0 cm
Australian National Gallery 1984.587

11. Ceremonial betel-nut bag
Sumbanese people, east Sumba, Indonesia,
early 20th century
Cotton, beads
Bead threading
56.0 x 35.0 cm
Australian National Gallery 1986.1248

11.

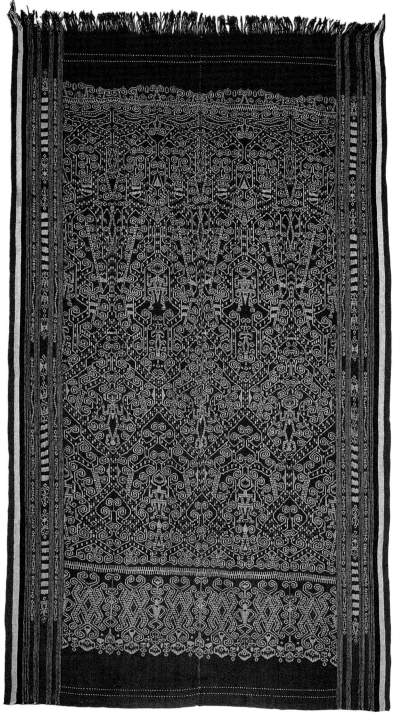

12.

13.

12. Ceremonial cloth *(pua kumbu)*
Iban people, Layar River, Sarawak,
Malaysia, early 20th century
Handspun cotton, natural dyes
Warp ikat
222.0 x 126.0 cm
Australian National Gallery 1984.611

13. (detail) Ceremonial shawl *(Pha biang)*
T'ai Phuan people, Xieng Khouang, Laos,
early 20th century
Silk, cotton, natural dyes
Supplementary weft weave
236.0 x 42.0 cm
Australian National Gallery 1986.1922

14. Ceremonial hanging *(pori situtu')*
Toraja people, Rongkong district,
central Sulawesi, Indonesia, 19th century
Handspun cotton, natural dyes
Warp ikat
157.0 x 260.0 cm
Australian National Gallery 1981.1126

14.

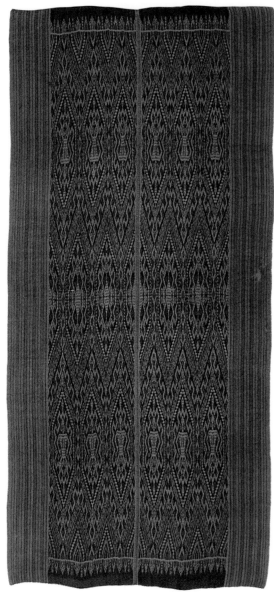

15.

15. Ceremonial textile *(tawit'ng doyo)*
Benuaq people, east Kalimantan, Indonesia,
19th century
Doyo fibre *(Curculigo latifolia)*, natural dyes
Warp ikat
207.0 x 98.0 cm
Australian National Gallery 1985.386

16. Ceremonial hanging *(palepai)*
Paminggir people, Kalianda district,
Lampung, Sumatra, Indonesia, 19th century
Handspun cotton, natural dyes
Supplementary weft weave
64.0 x 286.0 cm
Australian National Gallery 1985.611
Purchased with assistance from
James Mollison, 1985

17. Ceremonial textile *(tampan)*
Paminggir people, Lampung, Sumatra,
Indonesia, 19th century
Handspun cotton, natural dyes
Supplementary weft weave, twining
70.2 x 65.0 cm
Australian National Gallery 1981.1105

16.

17.

18.

18. Royal horse blanket
Tetum people, south Belu region, Timor,
Indonesia, early 20th century
Handspun cotton, silk, natural dyes, kapok
Supplementary weft wrapping, warp ikat,
quilting
104.0 x 215.0 cm
Australian National Gallery 1989.846

19. Woman's skirt *(pha sin)*
Tai Daeng people, Sam Nuea region, Laos,
19th century
Silk, cotton, natural dyes
Weft ikat, supplementary weft weave
67.0 x 144.0 cm
Australian National Gallery 1986.1926

20. Ceremonial shawl *(pha biang)*
Tai Daeng people, Sam Nuea region, Laos,
19th century
Handspun cotton, silk, natural dyes
Supplementary weft weave
119.0 x 43.0 cm
Australian National Gallery 1986.1927

19.

20.

21. Sacred textile *(usap)*
Sasak people, Lombok, Indonesia,
19th century
Handspun cotton, natural dyes
Supplementary weft weave
45.5 x 58.2 cm
Australian National Gallery 1986.2454

22.

23.

22. Man's cloth *(hinggi kombu)*
Sumbanese people, east Sumba, Indonesia,
20th century
Cotton, natural dyes
Warp ikat, weft twining
304.0 x 127.0 cm
Australian National Gallery 1984.1240

23. Woman's skirt *(lau pahudu)*
Sumbanese people, Pau district, east Sumba,
Indonesia, early 20th century
Handspun cotton, natural dyes
Supplementary warp weaving, tan staining,
fringe, embroidery
155.0 x 58.5 cm
Australian National Gallery 1984.617

The Indianized World of Southeast Asia

The influence of India on the architectural and sculptural arts of Southeast Asia is well recognized. It can also be readily identified in the region's textile arts. The development of local kingdoms, particularly in the more central coastal and lowland regions of Southeast Asia, supported by Indic philosophies of state and religion, produced significant changes in textile types and new textile functions.

The hierarchy of the courts, with distinctions between royalty, ranks of nobility, merchants, soldiers, servants and slaves, is reflected in the different textiles worn. Luxury fabrics with specific reserved designs were made exclusively for royal use. A ranking of textile types and patterns indicated the subtle distinctions in court circles. Ways of wearing textiles also indicated social status. Honours were earned or bestowed in fine textiles, between ruler and loyal subjects, between the palace and its territorial chiefs.

In particular, the introduction of silk and the development of sericulture provided the basis in many parts of the region for these textile distinctions. The clothing of the lower orders and those remote from the court centres continued to be barkcloths and vegetable fibres. The often exotic and luminous qualities of silk textiles were restricted to those of high rank and considerable wealth. These luxury fabrics were often embellished with gold and silver thread.

Changes in loom technology, in particular the introduction of the reed or comb to facilitate the weaving of fine silk thread, contributed to the creation of weft-decorated fabric — weft ikat, supplementary thread brocades and weft stripes. These luxurious fabrics were not intended to indicate the older social divisions of village, clan and gender. Rather, the size, colour, intricacy and exclusiveness of the central designs and border patterns signified the status and position of the wearer.

There were also changes in the meaning of textiles. Textiles, parasols and canopies of rank became a prominent part of the ritual and regalia of the courts of Southeast Asia. The Indic religions, Hinduism and Buddhism, also inspired special textile forms — valances for temples and shrines, prayer flags, manuscript covers — often displaying religious iconography. Figures from the great Hindu epics and tales of the Lord Buddha, deities, naga-serpents and cosmic mandalas were incorporated into Southeast Asian textile imagery.

Opposite:
Performers from the royal Cambodian dance theatre in glittering formal court dress.

24. Woman's skirt *(pha sin)*
Tai Daeng people, Sam Nuea region, Laos,
19th century
Silk, cotton, natural dyes
Weft ikat, supplementary weft weave
67.0 x 94.2 cm
Australian National Gallery 1988.1650

25. Religious hanging *(kalaga)*
Burmese people, Taunggyi, Amarapura
region, Myanmar (Burma), 1911
Silk, velvet, paper, sequins, semiprecious
stones
Embroidery, appliqué
165.0 x 442.0 cm
Australian National Gallery 1977.112

26. Shrine hanging *(lamak)*
Balinese people, Kesiman (?), Badung district,
south Bali, Indonesia, early 20th century
Handspun cotton, natural dyes, mirror pieces
in brass mounts, sequins, gold ribbon
Supplementary warp weave, appliqué,
embroidery
163.0 x 42.0 cm
Australian National Gallery 1989.496

27. Ceremonial hanging and covering *(pidan)*
Khmer people, Takeo province, Cambodia,
early 20th century
Silk, natural dyes
Weft ikat
83.0 x 137.4 cm
Australian National Gallery 1992.220
Gift of Michael and Mary Abbott 1992

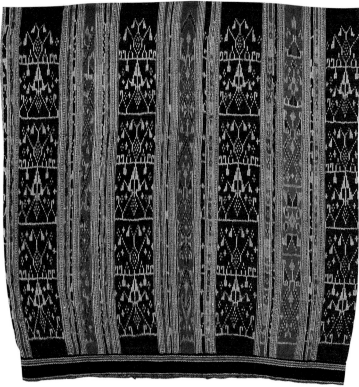
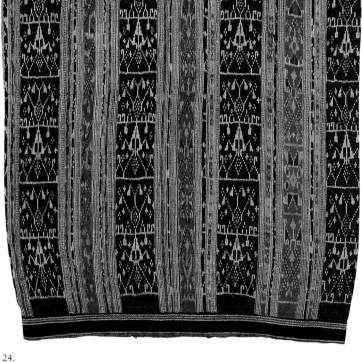

24.

26.

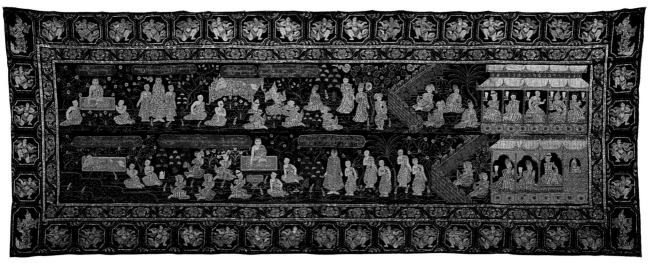

25.

27.

29.

28. Valance for a temple *(ider-ider)*
Balinese people, north Bali, Indonesia,
early 20th century
Cotton, silk, dyes, sequins, tinsel
Embroidery, appliqué
43.0 x 228.0 cm
Australian National Gallery 1987.1084
Gift of Michael and Mary Abbott 1987

29. Ceremonial cloth
Abung people (?), Kota Bumi district,
Lampung, Sumatra, Indonesia,
19th century
Bark-cloth, cotton, silk, dyes, gold metallic
thread, mirror pieces
Embroidery
65.0 x 65.0 cm
Australian National Gallery 1980.1629

30. Skirtcloth *(sampot hol)*
Khmer people, Cambodia, 19th century
Silk, natural dyes, metallic thread
Weft ikat, supplementary weft weave
91.8 x 292.8 cm
Australian National Gallery 1992.219
Gift of Michael and Mary Abbott 1992

31. (detail) Ceremonial skirtcloth
(pha khoie; chong kaben)
T'ai Lao people, Pakxe district, Laos,
19th century
Silk, natural dyes
Weft ikat
47.0 x 650.0 cm
Australian National Gallery 1987.1583

28.

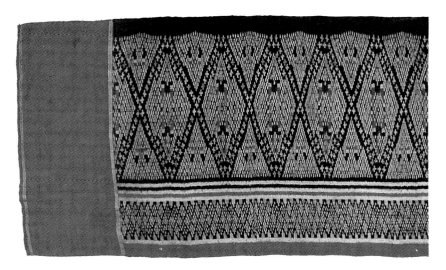

31.

30.

32. Ceremonial skirtcloth *(kain songket lemar)*
Malay people, Terengganu, Malaysia,
19th century
Silk, gold thread, natural dyes
Supplementary weft weave, weft ikat
103.4 x 213.0 cm
Australian National Gallery 1984.594

33. (detail) Ceremonial skirtcloth *(pha yok muang nakhon)*
Thai or Malay people, Nakhon Si Thammarat,
Thailand, late 19th century
Silk, gold thread, dyes
Continuous supplementary weft weave
94.0 x 278.0 cm
Australian National Gallery 1982.10
Gift of Mrs Winifred Thorvaldson 1982

34. Woman's ceremonial skirt *(tapis tua)*
Abung people, Lampung, Sumatra, Indonesia,
early 20th century
Cotton, vegetable dyes, gold thread,
metallic tinsel, sequins
Couched embroidery, appliqué
103.0 x 59.0 cm
Australian National Gallery 1980.729

35. Headcloth and shouldercloth
(tengkuluak; kain sandang)
Minangkabau people, Batu Sangkar district,
west Sumatra, Indonesia, 19th century
Cotton, silk, gold thread, natural dyes
Supplementary weft weave
271.0 x 74.0 cm
Australian National Gallery 1984.574

33.

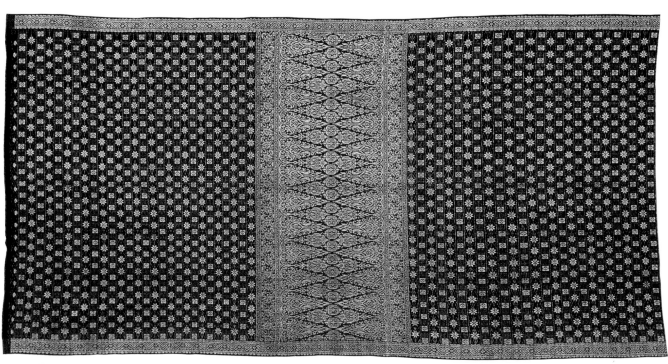

32.

35.

34.

Indian Textiles:
Prized Trading Commodities

Increasingly, foreigners were drawn into the Southeast Asian region in the quest for trade items — exotic jungle products such as resins and dyes, rare animal products ranging from birds' nests to rhinoceros horn, gold and silver, and foodstuffs. The well-known spices of eastern Indonesia, for example, attracted Arabs, Persians, Chinese, Indians and Europeans to the far edge of the region.

Crucial to trade throughout the region were textiles from the Indian subcontinent. While many of the tens of thousands of bales imported into Southeast Asia were plain cottons, a few types of expensive and beautiful cloth were in particularly great demand by the rulers of the region.

The silk double ikat *patola* — from Gujarat in west India — was the prize. It became the insignia of Southeast Asian princely houses, serving as a most prestigious status symbol and incorporated into the royal regalia. Occasionally tailored into garments or objects of ceremony, the five-metre diaphanous silks were more often displayed as hangings, canopies and palanquin covers for royal events.

Also greatly desired trade items were Indian painted and printed cottons. The fine Indian cotton fabric and the apparently miraculously bright dyes which appealed to traders from both East and West displayed a seemingly endless range of designs both geometric and figurative. The flexible nature of the mordant-painting technique, in which the designs are drawn onto the cloth in different mordants with a stylus before dyeing, and the Indian artisans' ability to respond to market demands meant that textiles of a great range of patterns arrived in the Southeast Asian region.

The designs included classical motifs presented in an Indian style, and patterns specifically recreated after the manner and to the tastes of particular audiences. While the Thai court of Ayutthaya demanded its own special style, other societies were much more eclectic, and even floral chintzes designed for the European market have found their way into the treasuries of remote island groups.

For it was not only the Indic court centres that appreciated the Indian imported cloth. Over centuries in remote parts of mainland and insular Southeast Asia, Indian cloths have become sacred clan treasures, magical objects and important status symbols.

Being such important objects, the Indian cloths inevitably became a source and inspiration for the region's textile makers. The individual motifs, the design elements and sometimes the layout structure often reflect a Southeast Asian interpretation of a valued heirloom.

Opposite:
An Ot Danum man wearing an heirloom Indian textile as a ceremonial loincloth in Kalimantan (Borneo).

36.

38.

36. (detail) Ceremonial furnishing cloth
(*pha lai yang*)
Coromandel coast, India; for Bangkok region,
Thailand, 18th century
Handspun cotton, natural dyes and mordants
Mordant and resist painting and printing
313.0 x 111.0 cm
Australian National Gallery 1984.621

37. (detail) Sacred heirloom (*ma'a*)
Gujarat, India; collected in Toraja region,
central Sulawesi, Indonesia, 17th century
Handspun cotton, natural dyes and mordants
Mordant painting, batik
102.0 x 534.0 cm
Australian National Gallery 1989.1329
Gift of Michael and Mary Abbott 1989

38. (detail) Ceremonial cloth and sacred heirloom in Indonesia (*patola*)
Gujarat region, India; collected in Lamaholot
region, Solor or Lembata, Indonesia,
18th century
Silk, natural dyes
Double ikat
111.0 x 500.0 cm
Australian National Gallery 1984.3184

37.

39. Sacred heirloom *(ma'a)*
Coromandel coast, India; collected in Toraja
region, central Sulawesi, Indonesia,
18th century
Handspun cotton, natural dyes and mordants
Mordant painting, batik
223.0 x 175.0 cm
Australian National Gallery 1987.1074
Gift of Michael and Mary Abbott 1987

40. Ceremonial parasol for royalty *(payung ?)*
north-west India; collected in Java, Indonesia,
19th century
Silk velvet, gold thread, sequins, tinsel,
semiprecious stones
Couched embroidery, appliqué
85 cm radius
Australian National Gallery 1987.1545

41. Skirtcloth *(kain songket)*
Malay people, Kelantan, Malaysia, 19th century
Silk, silver thread, natural dyes
Supplementary weft weave
97.5 x 166.6 cm
Australian National Gallery 1984.598

40.

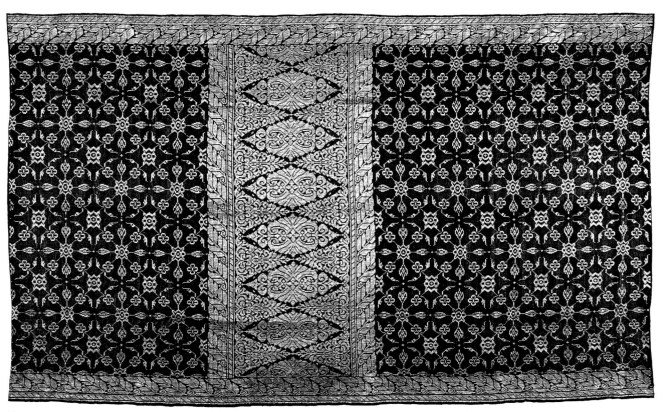

41.

42.

42. (detail) Ceremonial skirtcloths
(pha khoie; chong kaben)
T'ai Lao people, Pakxe district, Laos,
19th century
Silk, natural dyes
Weft ikat
89.0 x 316.0 cm
Australian National Gallery 1989.2252

43. (detail) Waistcloth or shouldercloth
(kain lemar)
Malay people, Terengganu, Malaysia,
19th century
Silk, natural dyes
Weft ikat
86.0 x 427.0 cm
Australian National Gallery 1984.593

44. Sacred heirloom textile
(ma'a or *mawa; mbesa)*
Toraja people, central Sulawesi, Indonesia,
early 20th century
Cotton, dyes
Painting, drawing, block printing
374.0 x 89.0 cm
Australian National Gallery 1983.3684

45. (detail) Ceremonial cloth
(kain nyulam)
Malay people, Palembang region,
south Sumatra, Indonesia, 19th century
Silk, gold thread, sequins
Embroidery, stitch-resist dyeing
83.5 x 190.0 cm
Australian National Gallery 1989.1495

43.

44.

45.

46.

47.

46. Ceremonial textile *(geringsing petang desa cecempakan)*
Balinese people, Tenganan village, Bali, Indonesia, early 20th century
Handspun cotton, natural dyes
Double ikat
176.0 x 61.0 cm
Australian National Gallery 1980.725

47. (detail) Breast cloth *(slendang; kemben)*
Javanese people, central region, Java, Indonesia, 19th century
Handspun cotton, natural dyes
Batik
58.8 x 248.5 cm
Australian National Gallery 1988.1545

48. Ceremonial cloth *(pua sungkit)*
Iban people, Sarawak, Malaysia, 19th century
Handspun cotton, natural dyes
Supplementary weft wrapping
204.0 x 97.0 cm
Australian National Gallery 1982.2304

48.

49.

49. Man's shawl *(semba)*
Endeh people, central Flores, Indonesia,
19th century
Cotton, natural dyes
Warp ikat
264.0 x 153.0 cm
Australian National Gallery 1984.581

50. Woman's skirt and ceremonial exchange object
(petak haren; kewatek nai telo)
Lamaholot people, south Lembata, Indonesia,
19th century
Handspun cotton, natural dyes
Warp ikat
167.0 x 72.0 cm (cylinder)
Australian National Gallery 1984.1219

51. Woman's ceremonial skirtcloth *(tapis inu)*
Paminggir people, Lampung, Sumatra, Indonesia,
19th century
Handspun cotton, silk, natural dyes
Warp ikat, embroidery
121.8 x 126.5 cm
Australian National Gallery 1989.1490

50.

51.

Chinese Influences: Trade and Migration

China had far less direct influence than India on Southeast Asia. However, Chinese traders, seeking forest and sea products for which the region was renowned, brought exchange objects highly valued within Southeast Asia. In particular, glazed ceramics and silk, both thread and fabric, were in great demand, and entered the treasuries of many wealthy families.

Although records of this trade exist, few examples of Chinese woven silks survive in insular Southeast Asia. However, in Laos and Thailand, Chinese brocades formed the basis for many royal garments, including shoulder sashes and skirts.

The elaborate collar that is a spectacular feature of Chinese dress was clearly much admired, and throughout Southeast Asia variations on the cloud-collar or phoenix-collar abound. In particular, court and theatrical costumes feature large multi-layered and many-lobed collars. These often form peaks at the shoulders which echo the form of bejewelled gold arm-bands.

Chinese men had settled in Southeast Asia over centuries, forming alliances with local women. In some parts of the region, for instance on the Malay peninsula, in southern Sumatra and on the north coast of Java, the mestizo communities that were formed — the Peranakan or Baba Chinese — developed their own distinctive textile traditions. These display a blend of the features of Chinese dress and those of the local groups into which the immigrants married. The Baba Chinese wedding costume and regalia incorporated Malay-inspired accessories and hangings with Chinese imperial-style gowns. These are decorated in fine embroidery in both couched gold, and satin and Peking-knot silks. The fine beadwork became a distinctive feature of the Baba Chinese communities.

On the north coast of Java, Chinese designs and well-known motifs were combined with the local Javanese decorative technique — batik — to produce the distinctive Peranakan or Nonya batik cloths. Gaily patterned with flowers, butterflies and Chinese mythical creatures, these fabrics became a popular item of trade throughout the whole of Southeast Asia, and the designs of many of the region's modern factory-printed textiles are based on the batiks of these mestizo Chinese communities. Some textiles, however, were not made for trade, but for particular use within the Peranakan Chinese communities. Embroidered religious hangings were replaced with batik ones for temple and domestic ceremonies.

Many of the silk embroidery traditions of Southeast Asia must have been inspired by fine Chinese items. So too may the rare tapestry weave traditions of the region, as the technique is most prominent in areas lying on trade routes, for instance Burma and the Sulu Archipelago in the far south of the Philippines. Although the designs are distinctively local, their inspiration may have been the spectacular *kesi* weaves of the Chinese courts.

A Lao queen and princess in Luang Prabang wearing jackets and skirts of richly worked Chinese brocade. The table covering is also embroidered with large Chinese dragons.

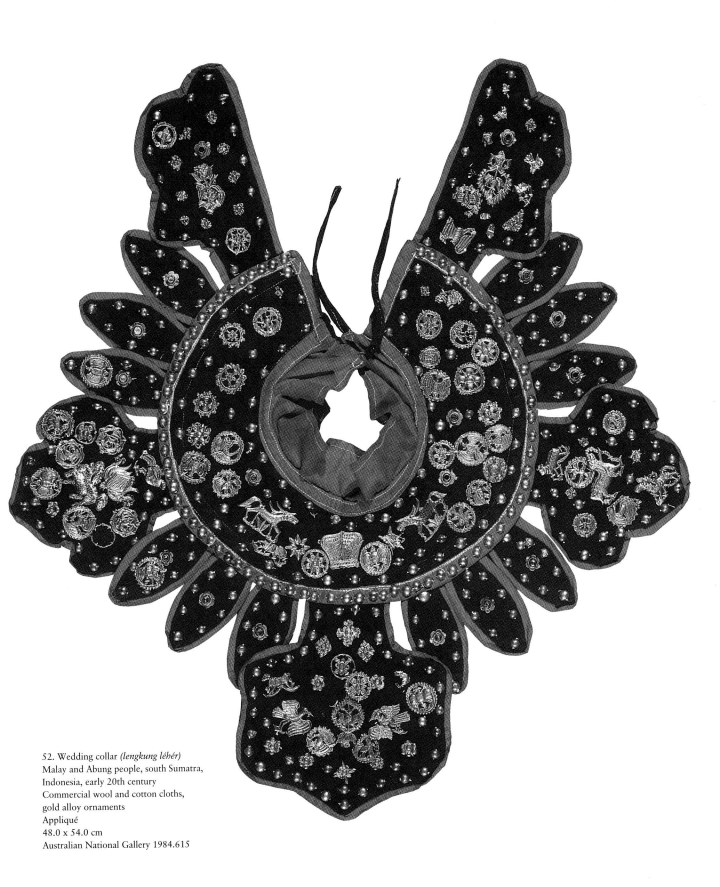

52. Wedding collar *(lengkung léhér)*
Malay and Abung people, south Sumatra,
Indonesia, early 20th century
Commercial wool and cotton cloths,
gold alloy ornaments
Appliqué
48.0 x 54.0 cm
Australian National Gallery 1984.615

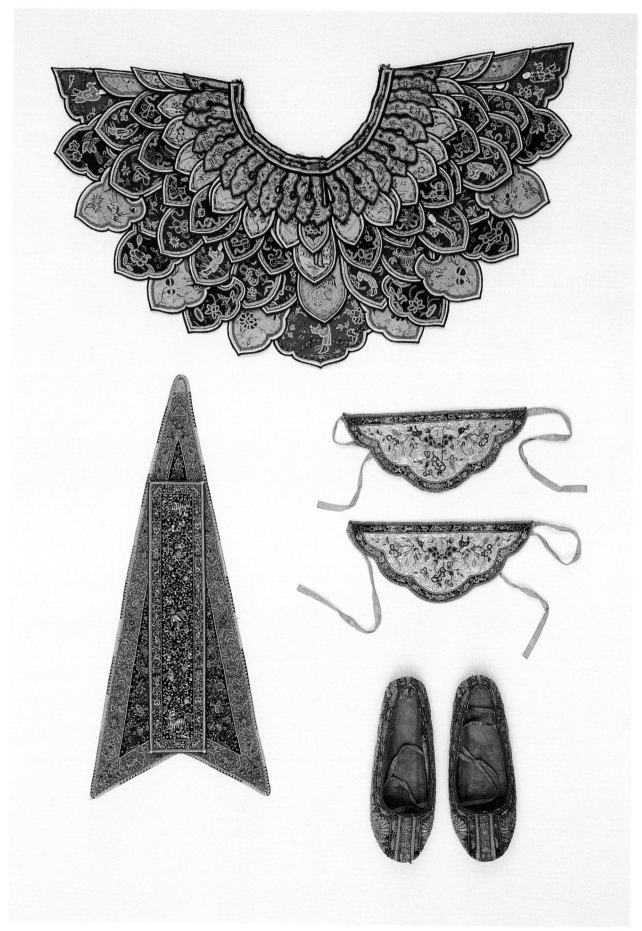

53.

53. Wedding slippers *(kasut manek)*;
handkerchief *(sapu tangan)*; kneepads; collar
Baba Chinese community, Malacca, Malaysia,
mid-19th century–early 20th century
Velvet, silk, cotton, sequins, beads, metallic
thread, sequins
Embroidery, beadwork
26.0 x 9.4 x 6.3 cm, 26.0 x 9.3 x 7.0 cm;
59.1 x 26.0 cm; 11.0 x 26.0 cm,
11.1 x 26.0 cm; 58.0 x 24.0 cm
Australian National Gallery 1992.221;
1992.224; 1992.222; 1992.223
From the Alice Smith Collection 1992

54. Canopy, hanging *(lelangit ?)*
Peranakan Chinese people, north-coast Java,
Indonesia, early 20th century
Cotton, natural dyes
Batik
255.0 x 270.0 cm
Australian National Gallery 1984.3091
Purchased with Gallery Shop Funds 1984

54.

55.

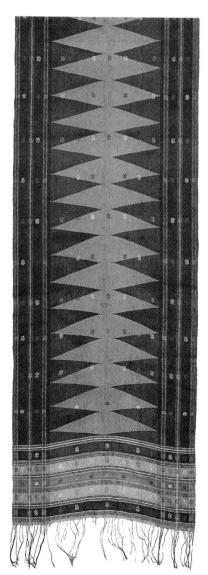

56.

55. Ceremonial hanging or banner
Peranakan Chinese community, Lasem, Java,
Indonesia, early 20th century
Cotton, natural dyes
Batik
205.8 x 84.0 cm
Australian National Gallery 1984.584

56. (detail) Shouldercloth or man's hipcloth
(salampé; pabasa)
Semawa or Bimanese people, Sumbawa,
Indonesia, early 19th century
Silk, dyes
Tapestry weave, supplementary weft weave
339.0 x 69.0 cm
Australian National Gallery 1984.1253

57.

57. (detail) Skirtcloth *(lùn-taya acheik)*
Burmese people, Mandalay or Amarapura
region, Myanmar (Burma), 19th century
Silk, natural dyes
Tapestry weave
107.0 x 396.0 cm
Australian National Gallery 1986.1252

58. Woman's ceremonial skirt
(malong landap)
Maranao people, Mindanao, Philippines,
early 20th century
Silk, dyes
Tapestry weave
175.0 x 86.0 cm
Australian National Gallery 1988.1593
Gift of Michael and Mary Abbott 1988

58.

Textiles for the New Faiths

Trade also attracted other foreigners into the region. The many traders from Arab countries, Persia and west India brought with them a new international religion — Islam. By the time the first Europeans penetrated the spice-producing islands of the Indonesian and Philippine archipelagoes, Islam had been established in many of the region's coastal courts and cities. The ruler of Malacca, on the Malay peninsula, probably the world's greatest entrepot at the time of the arrival of the Portuguese in the region, had already been converted.

European trading ships carried another international creed — Christianity — first Catholicism with the Portuguese, Spanish and French, and later Protestantism with the Dutch and English. As with Islam, conversions to Christianity also occurred in certain parts of the region, most prominently in the northern and central Philippines and eastern Indonesia.

One notable result of conversions to both Islam and Christianity was the change in notions of modesty throughout the region. In particular, bare breasts for women and bare heads for men were covered with new or adapted forms of traditional textiles. In particular, the man's characteristic square headcloth became a prominent feature of both everyday and formal wear, and gave rise to a wonderful variety of designs and methods of tying the simple item.

A Sultan of Pahang, Malaysia,
wearing a silk brocade headcloth distinctively
tied in his court style.

The demand for covering for the upper body encouraged the spread of tailored garments, and shirts and tunics of many shapes were adopted. Some developed from local warriors' jackets, or were simply a fine piece of fabric with a neck-hole along the seam to avoid cutting the selvages. Others were inspired by Mughal gowns much admired in the region's courts, while many were trimmed with braid and cut in European style.

Trousers were less popular. Although these garments often took their name from the Central Asian term *shalwa*, the different tailoring methods and cuts suggest a variety of models — Mughal or central Asian, European and Chinese. The menfolk of many communities, however, retained the checked skirtcloths, especially popular in coastal areas.

It appears that many of the earlier figurative motifs may have disappeared in favour of more schematic and geometric patterning in regions which adopted Islam. Floral motifs also appear to be popular. However, as in Mughal India, some Islamic cultures continued to incorporate figurative motifs, for example the well-known *wayang* images of Java and the widely popular *bouraq* winged horse. However, it is the designs formed from Arabic script which are among those most readily identified with Islamic communities. Appearing on headcloths, shawls, shrouds and hangings, the calligraphic designs are a feature of traditional rather than specifically religious occasions.

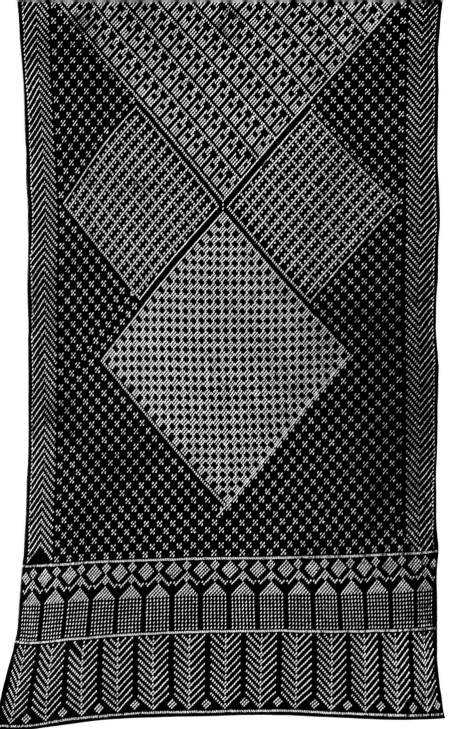

59.

59. (detail) Bridal veil
Egypt; Indonesia, early 20th century
Silk netting, silver ribbon
Embroidery
245.0 x 68.0 cm
Australian National Gallery 1986.1236

In the twentieth century in particular new design features, such as lacy or floral borders, have been incorporated into many textiles in all parts of Southeast Asia. Specifically European designs are, however, rarer, although many appear on the batik skirtcloths designed to be used by European and mestizo women in Java in the late nineteenth and early twentieth centuries, and on the gauzy piña pineapple fibre textiles of the northern Philippines.

However, flowers such as roses, irises and bluebells, modern conveyances such as steamships, aeroplanes and bicycles, and European mythical characters such as Red Riding Hood and Sleeping Beauty can also be found on Southeast Asian textiles. So too can messages and signatures in Roman script, the medium of modern education and mass communication in many parts of the region.

60.

61.

62.

60. Ceremonial hanging (*bi*)
Acehnese people, Sumatra, Indonesia,
early 20th century
Cotton, wool, silk, gold thread, sequins,
glass beads
Appliqué, couched embroidery, bobbin lace
64.0 x 208.0 cm
Australian National Gallery 1984.1986

61. Shouldercloth, shroud
(*kain batik tulisan Arab*)
Cirebon(?) Java; collected in Aceh, Sumatra,
Indonesia, 19th century
Handspun cotton, natural dyes
Batik, calendering, overdyeing
220.0 x 87.4 cm
Australian National Gallery 1987.347

62. (detail) Shouldercloth and waistcloth
(*kain songket*)
Malay people, Palembang, south Sumatra,
Indonesia, 19th century
Silk, gold thread, natural dyes
Supplementary weft weave
84.5 x 260.0 cm
Australian National Gallery 1989.1867

63. Man's headcloth (*pis siyabit*)
Tausug people, Sulu archipelago, Philippines,
early 20th century
Silk, dyes
Tapestry weave
88.0 x 77.0 cm
Australian National Gallery 1984.1215

63.

64.

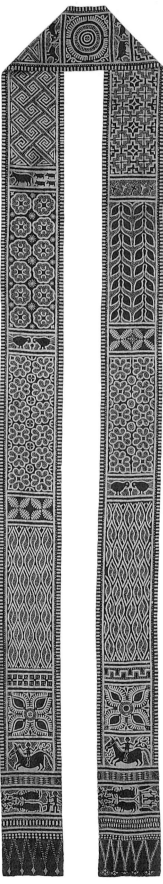

65.

64. Man's headcloth *(ikat kepala; tengkuluk; tengkolok)*
Malay people, Palembang region, Sumatra, Indonesia, 19th century
Silk, gold metallic thread, vegetable dyes
Supplementary weft weave, weft ikat
86.0 x 84.0 cm
Australian National Gallery 1980.1631

65. Sacred ceremonial cloth *(sarita)*
van Vlissingen & Co., Helmond, Netherlands; for Toraja region, central Sulawesi, Indonesia, late 19th–early 20th century
Cotton, indigo dyes
Paste-resist dyeing
487.0 x 17.6 cm
Australian National Gallery 1980.1653

66. Ceremonial cloth *(kain songket)*
Poetoe Menmatera Made Wirija, Bali, Indonesia, *c.*1920
Silk, gold thread
Supplementary weft weave
101.5 x 153.8 cm
Australian National Gallery 1989.405

66.

67.

67. Skirtcloth *(kain sarong)*
Lien Metzelaar, Pekalongan, Java, Indonesia,
c.1905
Cotton, natural dyes
Batik
104.0 x 103.0 cm (cylinder)
Australian National Gallery 1981.1138

68. Ceremonial skirtcloth *(kré tahan luji)*
Semawa people, west Sumbawa, Indonesia,
early 20th century
Cotton, silver ribbon, dyes
Embroidery
125.0 x 185.0 cm
Australian National Gallery 1987.1097
Gift of Michael and Mary Abbott 1987

68.

69.

70.

69. Man's trousers *(sawal)*
B'laan or Bagobo people, Mindanao,
Philippines, 19th century
Abaca fibre *(Musa textilis)*, cotton, dyes
Cross-stitch embroidery
47.0 x 51.0 cm
Australian National Gallery 1984.1229

70. Man's ceremonial trousers *(seluar)*
Malay people, Terengganu, Malaysia,
19th century
Silk, cotton, gold thread, natural dyes
Weft ikat, supplementary weft weave, needle
weaving
71.0 x 79.0 cm
Australian National Gallery 1984.1095

71. Woman's ceremonial tunic *(baju kurung)*
Malay people, Palembang, south Sumatra,
Indonesia, early 20th century
Velvet, silk, gold thread, sequins
Embroidery, couching
95.0 x 133.0 cm
Australian National Gallery 1989.1865

72. Ceremonial jacket *(baju telepok)*
Malay people, Malaysia,
late 19th century
Cotton, gold leaf
Gluework
50.0 x 105.0 cm
Australian National Gallery 1984.596

73. Woman's shirt *(albong* or *umpak)*
B'laan or Bagobo people, Mindanao,
Philippines, early 20th century
Cotton, beads
Appliqué
40.0 x 121.0 cm
Australian National Gallery 1986.2118

71.

72.

73.

Batik: One Technique, Many Design Sources

All Southeast Asian traditional textiles have changed over time in response to new and different materials, design formats, motifs and functions. The batik textiles of Java provide very clear instances of how this process of change has occurred in only one textile form.

Hand-drawn batik is a comparatively uncommon technique in most of Southeast Asia. On the mainland it is the technique used to pattern the hemp base-cloth of the pleated skirts of the Hmong of Laos, Thailand and Burma. In a few isolated parts of the Indonesian islands of Sulawesi and Java a simple form of paste-resist batik was used to inscribe bold schematic shapes on ritual hangings.

However, the batik for which the island of Java has become nationally and internationally famous appears to be a relatively recent development, an amazingly successful response to the mordant-dyed Indian cotton imports which flooded into Southeast Asia. This batik is performed with a pen-like *canting*, an instrument which controls the flow of molten wax from a tiny reservoir onto the smooth surface of a woven fabric. As a result, great detail of design and intricacy of pattern can be achieved by a skilled artisan. Although this growth of batik production — for local use and the export trade — may be only four hundred years old, these resist-dyed textiles reflect the major influences on the whole region's textiles.

Each region of Java makes recognizably different batik, based on local aesthetics, preferred design types and available dye materials. The rich reds of Lasem and the island of Madura contrast with the deep blues and dark browns of the central Javanese principalities and the stark white and cream grounds of the Cirebon style. Subject matters differ between the traditional sultanates of the island: measured geometric configurations are favoured by the courts of Solo (Surakarta) and Yogyakarta, while silhouettes of mythical figures and fantastic creatures in rocky landscapes and ordered friezes abound on Cirebon court cloths.

In one region, different local communities may produce distinctively different cloths for use within their own circles. In the north-coast batik town of Pekalongan the descendants of intermarriage between foreign traders and immigrants and local women display different customs and religious affiliations. The women of the Peranakan Chinese community, for example, favour bright multicoloured skirtcloths, the wide range of hues often being achieved through additional painting of dyes onto small areas of the design. Their motifs are often drawn from classical Chinese sources — dragons, phoenixes, *kilin* lion-dogs, peonies and butterflies are particularly popular. The descendants of Arab traders of course also wore batik, favouring non-figurative designs, often based on the stripes and grids of woven textiles. For weddings and other festive occasions the north-coast communities embellished their batik cloths with gold-leaf gluework or couched metallic thread embroidery.

The Indo-European women, descendants of Dutch traders and officials, were also prominent in batik production in the late nineteenth century and the first half of the twentieth century. Their creations displayed not only specifically European motifs such as lace and irises but also contemporary fashions in art, and floral motifs were transformed following the current Art Nouveau style. Even as recently as World War II, when Java was occupied by the Japanese army, new batik forms developed: the then scarce fine cotton fabrics were covered with intricate patterning, sometimes in the morning-evening *pagi-sore* style which displayed a distinctly different design in each half of one cloth. Japanese-inspired motifs, including flowers, birds and fans, were also incorporated.

As with other Southeast Asian traditional textiles, it is women who apply the *canting* pen to achieve these marvellous designs. With the introduction in the mid-nineteenth century of a hand-held metal block cap for applying the wax more quickly to the cloth's surface, men were recruited to perform batik work. This change in gender specialization is reflected all over Southeast Asia, where the traditional functions and meaning of textiles have been superseded by commercial considerations.

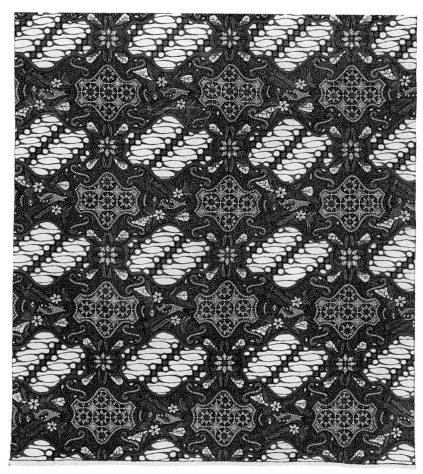

74.

74. (detail) Skirtcloth *(kain panjang)*
Javanese people, Yogyakarta, Java, Indonesia,
early 20th century
Cotton, natural dyes
Batik
109.5 x 252.0 cm
Australian National Gallery 1984.3114
Purchased from Gallery Shop Funds 1984

75. Hanging, banner
Cirebon region, Java, Indonesia,
late 19th century
Cotton, natural dyes
Batik
106.5 x 260.0 cm
Australian National Gallery 1984.3101
Purchased from Gallery Shop Funds 1984

76. Woman's skirt *(kain sarong)*
Peranakan Chinese people, north-coast Java,
Indonesia, late 19th century
Cotton, natural dyes
Batik, hand painting
111.5 x 101.0 cm
Australian National Gallery 1987.1063

77. Skirtcloth *(kain sarong)*
J. Jans, Pekalongan, Java, Indonesia, *c.*1905
Cotton, natural dyes
Batik
105.0 x 223.5 cm
Australian National Gallery 1984.3169

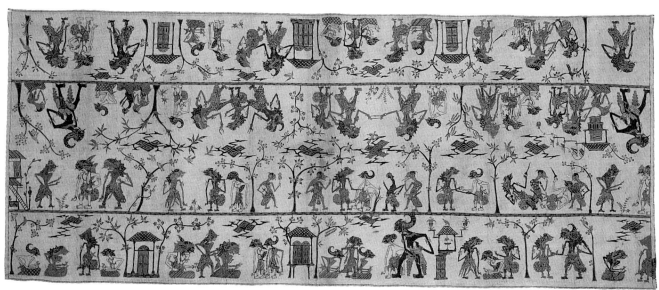

75.

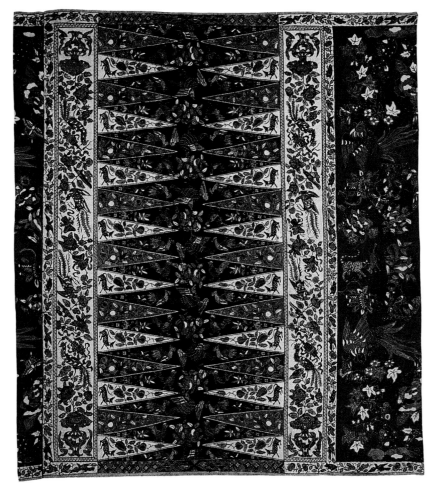

76.

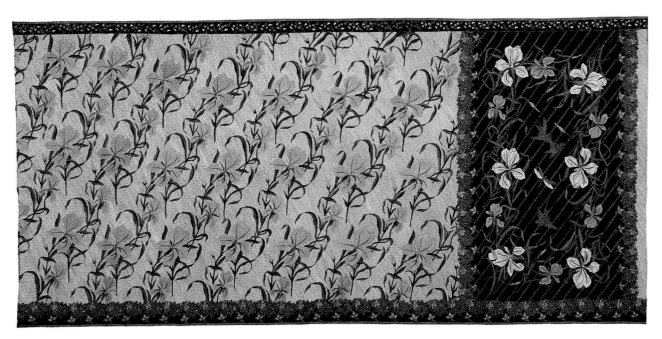

77.

78. Ceremonial skirtcloth *(kain panjang kauman)*
Peranakan Arab people, Pekalongan, Java, Indonesia, mid–20th century
Cotton, dyes, tinsel, sequins
Batik, embroidery
106.0 x 254.0 cm
Australian National Gallery 1984.3130
Purchased with Gallery Shop Funds 1984

79. Woman's skirtcloth *(kain panjang jawa hokokai)*
Peranakan Chinese people, north-coast Java, Indonesia, *c.*1945
Cotton, dyes
Batik
107.5 x 276.0 cm
Australian National Gallery 1984.3140
Purchased with Gallery Shop Funds 1984

78.

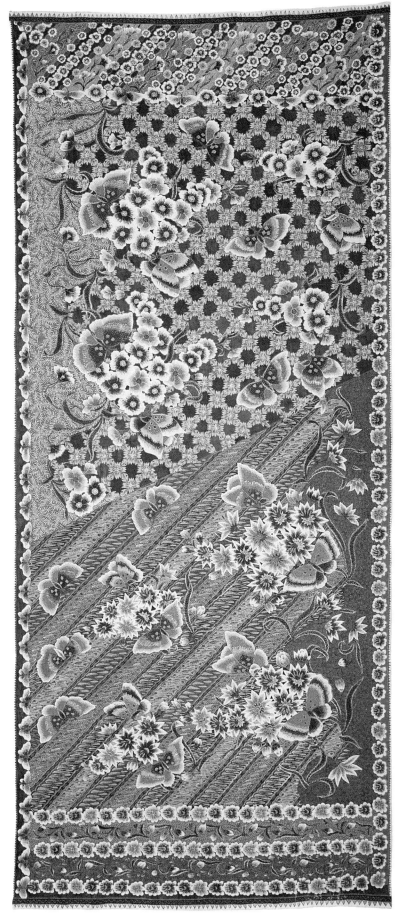

79.

Glossary of Technical Terms

abaca—A 'hard' fibre obtained from the leaf sheaths of the wild banana plant, *Musa textilis*.

aniline dyes—Aniline is a chemical substance derived from coal-tar. Discovered in 1856, it was the first synthetic dyestuff. It is sometimes used as a general term for synthetic or chemical dyes.

appliqué—The superimposition of areas of accessory fabric on a ground fabric, usually by stitching, for patterning purposes.

backstrap tension loom— A two-bar frameless loom with a backstrap, belt or wooden yoke passing around the weaver's back and secured to the breast-beam. The weaver controls the tension of the warp yarns by leaning forwards or backwards against the strap, while at the other end of the warp, another beam, known as the warp-beam, is held secure. It is also known as a back-tension loom or a body-tension loom.

bark-cloth—Smooth fabric made from a fibrous plant substance, usually inner bark or bast, which is softened, flattened and felted by soaking and beating.

bark-cloth beater—A bark-cloth beater is a mallet with a textured stone or wooden head, used to pound the softened bark fibres into a flat fabric.

basket weave—A style of weave in which the pattern has the appearance of matting or basketry.

batik—A resist-dyeing process in which a substance such as hot wax or rice paste is applied to the surface of fabric as a resist to dyes to form undyed areas of pattern. The resist is removed by boiling, melting or scraping after dyeing.

beading—A general term for the application of bead networks or strips of beads to a ground fabric. Also referred to as beadwork.

binding thread—The resist fibre (often strips of palm-leaf fibre) tied in patterns around the warp or weft threads. This prevents dye from entering those sections of the threads. After the dye process, the resist bindings are removed before the patterned threads are woven.

block printing— The use of carved wooden blocks to apply mordants or resist substances such as hot wax to the surface of woven cloth prior to dyeing.

bobbin—An article, usually a small rod, around which the weft thread is wound for insertion into the warp during weaving. Also a small pin of wood, with a notch, used in lace-making.

bobbin lace—Interlaced fabric made by manipulating groups of many separate threads by means of attached bobbins. The work is usually done on a pillow, hence the alternative term, pillow lace.

braid—A general term to describe a flat, decorative, woven or plaited tape or band used particularly to trim borders.

brocade—A general term referring to the patterning of woven fabric by means of supplementary threads.

It is usually applied to silk fabric richly patterned with gold or silver weft thread.

burnish—Make shiny by rubbing with a hard, smooth object.

calendering—A general term for polishing or glazing fabric.

canting—The Javanese name for a small batik tool consisting of a wooden handle with a copper reservoir from which a spout or spouts permit the controlled application of the molten wax to the cloth surface.

cap—The Javanese term for a metal stamp, usually constructed of strips of sheet copper, used in the batik process to apply molten wax to the cloth surface.

chintz—A mordanted and dyed cotton textile of Indian origin, although in English the term is generally applied to highly glazed, floral-printed cotton.

commercial fibres—Threads spun by machine. These include natural fibres such as cotton and silk and synthetic fibres.

complementary warp weaving—A woven fabric structure in which two sets of yarn elements in the warp are co-equal. In warp-faced fabric this weaving method may produce an identical pattern on both sides of the cloth.

continuous circulating warp—A set of warp threads or partially woven cloth, which make a continuous circle around the breast beam and warp beam. When the completed cloth is removed from the loom, it also is circular.

continuous supplementary weft (weaving)— Supplementary weft patterning in which the extra ornamental weft threads are carried back and forth across the full width of the cloth.

cotton— Fibre from the floss of the seed heads of cotton shrubs of the *Gossypium* family.

couching—A method of embroidery in which decorative threads are laid on the surface of the cloth and tacked in position with small stitches, which may themselves be arranged or coloured to create a pattern.

crochet lace— Open fabric formed by looping together threads with a hooked instrument.

cross-stitch—An embroidery style in which two flat stitches of equal length cross the same small area of ground fabric at opposite angles.

cut-and-drawn thread—A type of openwork embroidery which depends on the cutting and withdrawing of yarn from a woven ground fabric, and the stitching of the remaining threads and edges into decorative patterns. Also known as drawn threadwork.

damask—A general term applied to fabrics patterned by floating weaves dissimilar on each surface.

discontinuous fabric—A fabric woven in such a manner that it is removed from the loom as a non-circulating, flat rectangle. The manner of warping the loom through a comb usually results in a discontinuous length of fabric.

discontinuous supplementary weft (weaving)— Supplementary weft weaving in which extra weft threads are worked back and forth across limited areas of warp to shape pattern units.

double ikat—The ikat resist-dyeing process applied

separately to both warp and weft threads. The fabric is woven to achieve a balanced plain or tabby weave so that the patterning of both sets of loom threads emerges.

drop-weight spindle—A small hand-held rod weighted with a disc (spindle-whorl) which is allowed to spin freely from some height, to twist the fibre into thread.

dyestuffs—Materials used to colour threads or fabric. True dyes penetrate the fabric and bind to the fibres.

embroidery—Accessory stitches used to decorate or embellish a fabric, usually by means of needlework.

fabric—A generic term for all fibrous constructions.

felt, felting—A process of producing a firm fabric from the matting and adherence of a mass of fibres lying indiscriminately in all directions by mechanical processes such as pressure, moisture and pounding.

fibres—A general term referring to strands of plant or animal tissue, of naturally limited length, used in the construction of fabrics. 'Twisted fibres' refers to the twisting of two or more strands of unspun fibrous material.

field—The design element on a textile which contains a wide and often repetitive pattern. While usually occupying a central place in a design structure, the field on some Southeast Asian textiles may be divided by a head-panel.

flannel—Woven woollen fabric imported into Southeast Asia.

flat weave—A general term applied to carpets and rugs woven by a tapestry weave or weft wrapping process rather than a knotting technique which produces a tufted pile surface.

floating threads—Warp or weft threads travelling over or under two or more of the opposite elements.

foot-braced loom—A two-bar frameless loom, with one bar secured to a backstrap for controlling tension and the other bar braced against the weaver's feet. It is one type of backstrap tensionloom.

foundation weave—The basic woven structure of a fabric over which any supplementary elements float. This is usually a one-over-one-under tabby weave, also known as ground weave.

frame loom—A type of non-mechanical loom in which a wooden frame permits the tension on the warp threads to be regulated by the beams without the need for the backstrap operation of the earlier types of loom. The heddles are opened by foot pressure on pedals.

fringe—An ornamental border of loose or twisted threads, usually the unwoven warp ends remaining at each end of a length of fabric when the textile is removed from the loom and the warp is severed.

gauze—A general term applied to light, sheer or open fabrics.

gluework—The application of a glue or a viscous substance to the surface of a fabric to enable decorative elements to be attached.

gold thread—Thread formed from finely beaten gold ribbon usually wrapped around a core fibre.

ground, ground weave—The background weave or foundation of the fabric into which supplementary elements are interlaced.

handloom—Loom operated manually and not by a machine.

handspun cotton—Cotton thread made locally using simple non-mechanical apparatus such as a spindle or a spinning-wheel.

handspun thread—Locally grown animal or plant fibres, usually cotton or silk, spun into yarn by hand, using a spindle or a spinning-wheel.

head-panel—A section of different patterning which divides the field pattern on certain design structures of Southeast Asian textiles.

heddle—An essential feature of a loom which produces shed openings, through which the weft threads are inserted during the weaving process. In Southeast Asia it usually consists of a wide rod (heddle rod) to which selected sets of warp threads are attached by loops of yarn. These loops of yarn are sometimes also known as heddles.

heddle-sticks—Additional rods used to select particular warp threads for the purpose of creating the pattern. They are also known as shed-sticks. A supplementary weft is inserted in the sheds they are used to create.

hemp—Bast fibres obtained from the wild marijuana plant, *Cannabis sativa.*

ikat—The resist-dyeing process in which designs are reserved in warp or weft yarns by tying off small bundles of yarns with palm-leaf strips or similar materials to prevent the penetration of dye. For each colour, additional tying or partial removal of the bindings is required. After the last dyeing, all bindings are removed and the yarns are ready for weaving.

indigo—The blue-black dye derived from plants of the *Indigofera* and *Marsdenia* species, by producing an active precipitate from the reaction of the leaves with an alkaline solution.

Jacquard loom—A loom incorporating the Jacquard punched card apparatus, invented in the early nineteenth century, which mechanically opens the warp sheds in intricate repetitive patterns. Usually the warps are lifted and the shuttles are thrown also by mechanical means.

kesi—A Chinese term for weft-faced, often slit-tapestry weaving.

kit—The term applied to continuous supplementary weft weaving in northern Thailand and Laos.

knotting—A fabric formed by tying free-hanging sets of threads around adjacent threads, in combinations of structurally identical knots.

lac—The resinous droppings of the lac insect, *Coccus lacca*, deposited under the bark of certain trees. It is a popular source of red dye in mainland Southeast Asia. Also known as stick lac.

lace—A general term for an open, usually finely worked fabric.

loom—Apparatus on which sets of yarn are interlaced, by shed openings, to produce woven cloth.

machine printing—The process of printing designs in dyes or pigments onto a cloth surface by mechanical means, usually employing copper-plates or rollers onto which the patterns are etched or engraved.

macramé—A general term for ornamental knotwork. More specifically the term refers to an ornamental fringe of knotted threads.

matting—An often somewhat rigid fabric constructed of interlocking fibres which are not woven on a loom with shed openings. Also known as basketry.

metallic thread—Worked metals, especially gold and silver, are used to fashion thread either in the form of wire or flat metal ribbon, or wound around a core of other fibre. The metallic thread is used as a weaving and embroidery element.

mica—Thin, flexible, transparent and glittering scales of silicate found naturally and used to decorate garments in Southeast Asia. Mica has largely been replaced by mirror pieces.

mirror-work—Rounds cut from thin mirror glass, often lead-backed, or from mica, and sewn onto a base fabric with a framework of stitches.

mordant—A chemical which serves to fix a dye in or on thread or fabric by combining with the dyestuff to form an insoluble compound.

mordant block printing—A design in mordants applied to cloth by carved wooden blocks. The design remains fixed and the coloured pattern stands out against an undyed ground after the dye process.

mordant painting—A design in mordants painted onto a prepared cloth with a pen or stylus. The mordants will react with the dyes to produce a colourful pattern against an undyed ground.

Morinda citrifolia—A tree grown widely in Southeast Asia, the bark of the roots of which yield red or rust dye. It is known as *mengkudu, kumbu* or a related term.

natural dyes—Dyestuffs obtained from natural plant, animal and mineral substances.

needle braid—A decorative border or join achieved by interweaving threads with a needle.

needle weaving—A weaving technique in which the weft elements are inserted with the assistance of a needle. The needle may also be used to open the sheds.

net, netting—A general term for an open-textured, net-like fabric.

netted beadwork—The threading onto yarn of a large number of different coloured tiny beads in a regular pattern to form a variety of coloured designs in an open net-like fabric. This is then anchored onto a ground fabric with stitches.

over-dyeing—Dyestuffs of different colours used consecutively to achieve a darker, mixed colour.

painting—The application of mordants, dyestuffs or pigments to an object, usually to the surface of a fabric, or to unwoven threads.

palampore—A mordant-painted and sometimes batik resist-dyed Indian cotton fabric which usually features an elaborate flowering tree on a rocky mound. One genre of chintz.

panel—A section of a textile or a separate length of fabric. Not to be confused with a head-panel, a design element on certain Southeast Asian textiles.

paste-resist—A resist-dyeing process in which a thick paste is applied to the surface of the fabric and allowed to harden before the cloth is dyed.

patchwork—A decorative fabric assembled by seaming together many relatively small and more or less equivalent pieces of a number of different fabrics.

pattern-sticks—Sets of shed-sticks supplementary to the main heddles used to create other sheds for the purpose of decorative patterning. Mostly used for supplementary weft weaving, they may also be used to create supplementary warp patterning.

pigments—Colouring agents which stay on the surface of the fabric.

pilih—The term applied to continuous supplementary weft weaving in Borneo and Kalimantan.

piña—Threads obtained from the shredded leaves of the wild pineapple plant. Also the name of the cloth woven from these threads.

plaid—A checkered pattern achieved by weaving different sets of coloured warp and weft threads in recurring arrangements.

plaiting—A general term for the process of basketry and matting, in which fibres are interlaced to form fabric without the use of a loom with heddles, the elements being indistinguishable as warp and weft and all active at different times.

plangi—A resist-dyeing and patterning process in which areas of cloth are reserved from dye by being bound off with dye-resistant fibres before dyestuffs are applied. Patterns are usually built up from small circles.

prada—A term widely used in Southeast Asia for gold leaf gluework, the application of gold leaf or gold dust to the cloth surface.

rattan—Fibre from the stems of various climbing palms of the genus *Calamus*, used for matting and basketry.

rayon—A term for artificially made silk thread.

reed—A piece of loom apparatus consisting usually in Southeast Asia of fine bamboo slivers standing vertically between two horizontal bars. The reed acts as a warp-spacer and, when weaving, the weaver beats the reed against the newly inserted weft thread with her sword. It is also known as the comb.

resist-dyeing—Any process which employs dye-resistant materials to block the penetration of dyes onto or into selected areas of fabric or threads for the purpose of decorative patterning.

ribbon embroidery—An embroidery technique in which narrow flat ribbon thread, usually of beaten silver in Southeast Asia, is interlaced or stitched into a net or gauze-like fabric.

rickrack—Narrow zigzag braid used as trimming.

sappanwood—The wood of a small tree, *Caesalpinia sappan*, from which a red dyestuff is obtained.

satin-stitch—A simple, straight, flat stitch, circling through the fabric, which is often used to produce flat, smooth, patterned surfaces by laying a series of fairly long stitches parallel and close together.

selvage—The edges of a textile where the wefts encircle the outermost warp threads.

sequins—Small, shiny, usually metallic discs with a central hole. Also known as spangles.

sericulture—The rearing of silkworms and the production of raw silk.

shed—A temporary opening between two planes of warp threads, selectively separated, for the passage of the weft during the weaving process.

shed opener —A device used to open a shed through which the weft threads can be inserted during the weaving process.

shed-sticks —Rods or sticks used in conjunction with a main heddle to produce other often irregular sheds for supplementary thread patterning.

shuttle —A tool by which the weft is passed through the shed opening in the warp during weaving. In many cases in Southeast Asia the weft is wound onto a bobbin which is placed inside a shuttle case for weaving.

silk —Thread composed of filaments secreted by caterpillars. It is obtained from the cocoons of the cultivated mulberry silkworm, *Bombyx mori*, or other wild silk-insect sources.

silver thread —Thread formed from finely beaten silver ribbon, sometimes wrapped around a core fibre.

slit-tapestry weave —Tapestry weave in which the adjacent areas of colour are separated by slits in the woven fabric, achieved by repeatedly turning back the discontinuous weft threads around adjacent warps.

soga —A brown dye used in Javanese batik, derived from a combination of bark and wood from several trees. A major ingredient is the bark of the soga tree, *Peltophorum ferrigineum*.

songket —A widely used term in Southeast Asia for supplementary weft patterning usually denoting metallic thread as the major supplementary weft element.

spindle —A tool used for spinning thread. The hand spindle consists of a short rod weighted at the lower end with a disc (spindle-whorl). It is either let fall from a height to spin freely or spun with the lower point in a smooth concave receptacle.

spindle-whorl —A small disc through which the spindle-rod passes. It provides weight and balance during the spinning process.

spinning —The process of twisting together and drawing out massed short fibres into a continuous strand.

spinning-wheel —Apparatus consisting of a wheel turned by hand which rotates, via a belt, a spindle-rod around which the spun thread is twisted. In Southeast Asia this apparatus sits flush with the ground.

staining —A method of colouring small sections of pattern on fabrics after the weaving is completed, by the staining or daubing of dyes, usually of a fugitive nature.

stem-stitch —An embroidery stitch which moves forward on the front of the cloth and then part-way back on the underside of the cloth to start the next forward stitch on the top surface in a regular fashion. It is used to produce lines or outlines.

stick batik —A batik resist-dyeing process in which the resist substance is applied with a small stick or rod rather than a pen or block.

stumpwork —Raised couched metal thread embroidery which is worked over padding or a card cut to the shape of the pattern to achieve a three-dimensional effect.

sungkit —A term applied in Borneo and Kalimantan to weft wrapping. Elsewhere in Southeast Asia it is an alternative spelling and pronunciation of *songket*, supplementary weft weaving.

supplementary warp (weaving) —A decorative weaving technique in which an additional set of warp threads is woven into a textile to create an ornamental pattern additional to the ground weave.

supplementary weft (weaving) —A decorative weaving technique in which extra ornamental weft threads are woven into a textile between two regular wefts to create patterns additional to the ground weave.

sword —A smooth narrow wooden slat, inserted into newly opened sheds of warp threads and used to beat in each newly inserted weft.

synthetic dyes —Synthetic chemicals used as dyestuffs. Increasingly available since the first aniline dyes were discovered in the mid-nineteenth century.

synthetic fibres —A general term for artificially made fibres. More specifically the term refers to mechanically extruded thread; usually long, fine, structurally continuous filaments obtained by a chemical process from petroleum and coal-tar by-products.

tabby weave —The simplest basic interlacing of warp and weft threads in a one-over-one-under plain weave.

tablet weaving —A band weaving process in which warps are threaded through holes punched in tablets or cards which are turned to create shed openings for the weft to pass through.

tailor —A general term to describe the making of a garment by cutting and sewing.

tapestry weave —Weft-faced plain weave, with discontinuous wefts, usually of different colours, woven back and forth within their own pattern areas.

thread —A simple continuous aggregate of fibres that is suitable for textile construction. The composition of threads varies in Southeast Asia from single strands of fibrous material, untwisted but knotted to achieve length, to spun yarn which is plied or twined for added strength and thickness.

tie-dyeing —A general term for resist-dyeing processes applied to already woven fabric, in which areas of fabric are reserved from dyes by stitching *(tritik)* or binding with fibre *(plangi)*.

tinsel —Coarse decorative thread embellished with rough pieces of gold, silver or imitation metal leaf.

treadle loom —A loom in which the heddles are alternately opened by use of a foot-operated treadle. Also known as a foot-operated heddle loom.

tritik —A resist-dyeing and patterning process in which the cloth is stitched, gathered and tucked tightly before dyestuffs are applied so that dye cannot penetrate the reserved areas.

tuft —Short bunches of fibre secured in the basic fabric.

turmeric —A fugitive yellow dyestuff obtained from the rhizome of the *Curcuma domestica* plant.

twill weave —Weaving or cloth patterned by a regular diagonal alignment of floating threads.

twining —Two or more weft (or warp) elements worked together by spiralling around each other while encircling successive warps (or wefts).

vegetable dyes —Dyestuffs obtained from naturally occurring plant material.

vegetable fibres —Fibrous plant materials which can be used for the construction of thread and felted fabric.

velvet —A fabric characterized by a woven pile, imported into Southeast Asia.

voile —Thin semi-transparent woven fabric.

warp —Parallel threads that run longitudinally on the loom or cloth.

warp-beam —A board or rod which holds the warp threads in a frameless backstrap tension loom. It may be a flat board around which a discontinuous warp is rolled, or a bamboo roller for a continuous, circulating warp.

warp-faced —Woven fabric in which the warp threads conceal the weft.

warp ikat —The ikat resist-dyeing process applied only to the warp threads so that the warp threads are patterned before weaving. The fabric is woven to achieve a predominantly warp-faced weave.

warping —To wind or string the warp threads onto a frame or loom by laying out threads of equal length parallel to each other.

weaving —To interlace warp and weft threads in a specific order with the aid of apparatus, usually a loom, which facilitates shed openings.

weft —Traverse threads in a fabric that cross and interlace with the warp elements.

weft-faced —Woven fabric in which the weft threads conceal the warp.

weft ikat —The ikat resist-dyeing process applied only to the weft threads so that the weft threads are patterned before weaving. The fabric is woven to achieve a predominantly weft-faced weave.

weft twining —Two sets of threads worked together by spiralling around each other while encircling successive warps.

weft wrapping —The encircling or wrapping of passive warp elements by weft threads to create a pattern. The weft threads can be either the sole wefts in the fabric or supplementary to regular wefts in a ground weave. The weft threads, usually discontinuous, can be wrapped with the fingers, a pick or a needle. Known as *sungkit* in Borneo and *jok* in Laos and Thailand.

Selected Reading

HISTORICAL BACKGROUND

Bellwood, P. *Man's Conquest of the Pacific: The Prehistory of Southeast Asia and Oceania.* New York: Oxford University Press, 1979.

Bellwood, P. *Prehistory of the Indo-Malayan Archipelago.* Sydney: Academic Press, 1985.

Hall, K.R. *Maritime Trade and State Development in Early Southeast Asia.* Sydney: George Allen and Unwin, 1985.

Marr, D., and Milner, A.C. (eds.). *Southeast Asia in the 9th to 14th Centuries.* Singapore: Institute of Southeast Asian Studies, 1986.

Reid, A. *Southeast Asia in the Age of Commerce 1460-1680: Volume One, The Land Below the Winds.* New Haven: Yale University Press, 1988.

TEXTILES AND TRADE

Bühler, A., and Fischer, E. *The Art of the Patola.* 2 vols. Basel: Krebs, 1979.

Dubin, L.S. *The History of Beads.* New York: Harry N. Abrams, 1987.

Gittinger, M. *Master Dyers to the World.* Washington, DC: Textile Museum, 1982.

Guy, J. *Oriental Trade Ceramics in South-East Asia: Ninth to Sixteenth Century.* Singapore: Oxford University Press, 1986.

Irwin, J., and Schwartz, P. *Studies in Indo-European Textile History.* Ahmedabad: Calico Museum of Textiles, 1966.

Yoshioka, T., and Yoshimoto, S. *Sarasa of the World.* Kyoto: Kyoto Shoin, 1980.

SOUTHEAST ASIAN TEXTILES

Casal, G.S. *T'boli Art in its Socio-Cultural Context.* Manila: Ayala Museum, 1978.

Cheesman, P. *Lao Textiles: Ancient Symbols — Living Art.* Bangkok: White Lotus, 1988.

Cheo, Kim Ban. *A Baba Wedding.* Singapore: Eastern Universities Press, 1983.

Fraser-Lu, S. *Handwoven Textiles of South-East Asia.* Singapore: Oxford University Press, 1988.

Gittinger, M. *Splendid Symbols: Textiles and Tradition in Indonesia.* Washington, DC: Textile Museum, 1979.

Gittinger, M. (ed.). *To Speak With Cloth: Studies in Indonesian Textiles.* Los Angeles: Museum of Cultural History, University of California, 1989.

Hauser-Schäublin, B.; Nabholz-Kartaschoff, M.L.; and Ramseyer, U. *Textiles of Bali.* Singapore: Periplus, 1991.

Ho, W.M., *Straits Chinese Beadwork and Embroidery.* Singapore: Time Books International, 1987.

Holmgren, R.J., and Spertus, A. *Early Indonesian Textiles from Three Island Cultures.* New York: Metropolitan Museum of Art, 1989.

Lewis, P., and Lewis, E. *People of the Golden Triangle.* London: Thames and Hudson, 1984.

Maxwell, R. *Textiles of Southeast Asia: Tradition, Trade and Transformation.* Melbourne: Australian National Gallery/Oxford University Press, 1990.

Naenna, P. Cheesman. *Costume and Culture: Vanishing Textiles of Some of the T'ai Groups in Laos P.D.R.* Chiang Mai: Studio Naenna, 1990.

Newman, T.R. *Contemporary Southeast Asian Arts and Crafts.* New York: Crown Publishers, 1977.

Ong, E. *Pua: Iban Weavings of Sarawak.* Kuching: Atelier Sarawak, 1986.

Peacock, B.A.V. *Batek, Ikat, Pelangi and Other Traditional Textiles from Malaysia.* Hong Kong: Urban Council, 1977.

Peetathawatchai, V. *Folkcrafts of the South.* Bangkok: Housewives Voluntary Foundation, 1976.

Prangwatthanakun, S. and Cheesman, P. *Lan Na Textiles: Yuan, Lue, Lao.* Chiang Mai: Centre for the Promotion of the Arts and Culture, 1987.

Rubenstein, D.H. *Fabric Treasures of the Philippines.* Guam: ISLA Center for the Arts, University of Guam, 1989

Selvanayagam, G. Inpam. *Songket: Malaysia's Woven Treasure.* Singapore: Oxford University Press, 1990.

Sheppard, M. *The Living Crafts of Malaysia.* Singapore: Times Books International, 1978.

Solyom G., and Solyom, B. *Fabric Traditions of Indonesia.* Pullman: Washington State University Press, 1985.

THE ARTS OF SOUTHEAST ASIA

Barbier, J.P., and Newton, D. (eds.). *Islands and Ancestors: Indigenous Styles in Southeast Asia.* New York: Prestel, 1988.

Casal, G.S.; Jose, R.T.; Casino, E.S.; Ellis, G.R.; and Solheim, W.G. *The People and Art of the Philippines.* Los Angeles: Museum of Cultural History, University of California, 1981.

Chin, L. *Cultural Heritage of Sarawak.* Kuching: Sarawak Museum, 1980.

Feldman, J. (ed.). *The Eloquent Dead: Ancestral Sculpture of Indonesia and Southeast Asia.* Los Angeles: Museum of Cultural History, University of California, 1985.

Jessup, H. Ibbitson. *Court Arts of Indonesia.* New York: Harry N. Abrams, 1990.

Jumsai, Sumet. *Naga: Cultural Origins in Siam and the West Pacific.* Singapore: Oxford University Press, 1988.

Lowry, J. *Burmese Art.* London: Victoria and Albert Museum, 1974.

Ramseyer, U. *The Art and Culture of Bali.* Oxford: Oxford University Press, 1977.

Rodgers, S. *Power and Gold: Jewelry from Indonesia, Malaysia and the Philippines.* Geneva: Barbier-Müller Museum, 1985.

Sellato, B. *Hornbill and Dragon.* Jakarta: Elfaquitaine, 1989.

Sheppard, M. *Taman Indera: Malay Decorative Arts and Pastimes.* Singapore: Oxford University Press, 1972.

Taylor, P.M. *Beyond the Java Sea.* Washington, DC: National Museum of Natural History, 1991.